RECENT ADVANCES IN CRYPTOGRAPHY AND NETWORK SECURITY

Edited by **Pinaki Mitra**

Recent Advances in Cryptography and Network Security
http://dx.doi.org/10.5772/intechopen.71917
Edited by Pinaki Mitra

Contributors

Jingwei Hu, Ray Cheung, Rushdi Hamamreh, Mohamad Afendee Mohamed, N A Mahadi, A.I. Mohamad, M Makhtar, M F A Kadir, M. Mamat, Pinaki Mitra

Notice

Statements and opinions expressed in the chapters are these of the individual contributors and not necessarily those of the editors or publisher. No responsibility is accepted for the accuracy of information contained in the published chapters. The publisher assumes no responsibility for any damage or injury to persons or property arising out of the use of any materials, instructions, methods or ideas contained in the book.

First published in London, United Kingdom, 2018 by IntechOpen
IntechOpen is the global imprint of INTECHOPEN LIMITED, registered in England and Wales, registration number: 11086078, The Shard, 25th floor, 32 London Bridge Street
London, SE19SG – United Kingdom
Printed in Croatia

British Library Cataloguing-in-Publication Data
A catalogue record for this book is available from the British Library

Additional hard copies can be obtained from orders@intechopen.com

Recent Advances in Cryptography and Network Security, Edited by Pinaki Mitra
p. cm.
Print ISBN 978-1-78984-345-3
Online ISBN 978-1-78984-346-0

For EU product safety concerns:
IN TECH d.o.o., Prolaz Marije Krucifikse Kozulić 3, 51000 Rijeka, Croatia,
info@intechopen.com or visit our website at intechopen.com.

Meet the editor

Pinaki Mitra is currently an associate professor at the Department of Computer Science and Engineering, IIT Guwahati. He obtained his B. Tech in Computer Science and Engineering from Jadavpur University, Kolkata in 1987, India and his M. Tech in Computer Science and Engineering from the Indian Institute of Science Bangalore, India in 1989. He obtained his Ph.D. from the Simon Fraser University, Canada in 1994. He has worked on a project at the Department of Computer Science and Engineering, Jadavpur University. Subsequently, he joined the National Institute of Management, Kolkata, and served as an assistant professor. He joined IIT Guwahati in December, 2004. His research interests include cryptography, network security, computer graphics and multimedia.

Contents

Chapter 1

Introductory Chapter: Recent Advances in Cryptography and Network Security

Pinaki Mitra

Additional information is available at the end of the chapter

http://dx.doi.org/10.5772/intechopen.81283

1. Introduction

In the last few decades, we observed a significant development in the field of computing. Initially, we had mainframe systems. Subsequently, personal computers evolved. The physical size of both processors and storage got reduced. With the advent of new technology, the computing power and storage capability increased. In personal computers, we subsequently observed the amalgamation of parallel processing concepts with the development of multicore chips. But more importantly, the technology that developed rapidly was that of Internet and computer networks [1]. Personal computer interconnected via Internet provides significant computing facility to users. The interconnection is either wired or wireless. The size of these computing devices got further reduced with the advent of mobile computing. The handheld mobile devices provide significant computing facility to the users through wireless interconnection. As the computing technology evolved, there is a significant growth in the volume of communicated data across the network. The increased traffic causes delay in data transmission. So, there is necessity of data compression that can reduce the traffic significantly. Different coding and compression techniques for audio, image, video, text, and graphics data emerged to handle these problems. In audio, we have seen different compression schemes like MP3, AVI, etc. Image compression is achieved using JPEG. In video compression, there had been a series of developments in MPEG techniques. Text compression is achieved through different coding techniques like Huffman [2] encoding or Lempel-Ziv-Welch (LZW) encoding [3, 4].

Another problem that has to be addressed is the security and privacy of the huge amount of communicated information through either wired or wireless transmission media. We observed a significant development in the area of cryptography and network security [5]. The area of cryptography concerns secure communication between sender and receiver that should prevent the eavesdropper to tamper or intercept confidential data. Different encryption and

decryption techniques evolved for this purpose. They are broadly classified into two types: (a) symmetric-key and (b) public-key cryptosystems. In symmetric-key cryptography, the same key is shared between the sender and the receiver. But in public-key cryptography, the sender sends the encrypted data to the receiver using receiver's public key. The receiver decrypts the data using his/her own secret key. There are several cryptographic algorithms for both symmetric- and public-key cryptosystems. **Figure 1** depicts symmetric-key cryptosystem. **Figure 2** depicts public-key cryptosystem. In both figures, the sender is Alice and the receiver is Bob. The unencrypted message M is usually known as plain text. The encrypted message C is called cipher text or in short cipher.

Another important aspect of secure communication is that of nonrepudiation. This is achieved by means of digital signature. In public-key cryptosystem, the sender sends both message and the signature that is the encrypted version of the message with the private/secret key of the sender. **Figure 3**, illustrates the digital signature scheme where the digital signature $S = S_A(M)$ is the message encrypted with the secret key of Alice. The 2-tuple (S, M), i.e., the signature along with the message is transmitted to Bob. At the receiving end, Bob applies the public key of Alice to obtain $M' = P_A(S) = P_A(S_A(M))$ that is supposed be equal to M if the signature is valid. So Bob compares M′ and M and accepts if they are equal otherwise Bob rejects. There are several variations of signature schemes and many of them use cryptographic hash functions.

The similar notion of authentication is also used in image data. Several techniques related to that had evolved recently in digital water marking and steganography. Also, there had been a significant development in the field of authentication using biometric data.

With advent of quantum computers, there had been significant development in the area of postquantum cryptography. This is because several computationally difficult problems for classical computing model are susceptible to attacks in quantum computing model. Postquantum cryptographic algorithms had to handle these challenges.

In the area of network security, we had seen different new types of attacks with the advent of mobile computing technology where there are no fixed interconnections among mobile nodes. One frequent type of attack in particular is DDOS or distributed denial of service attack. This attack causes jamming of the network by flooding redundant packets across the network. There are several remedies that had been devised to counter these attacks. Typical information theoretic measures like *precision* and *recall* may be used to evaluate the performance of these remedial techniques with true positives, true negatives, false positives, and false negatives.

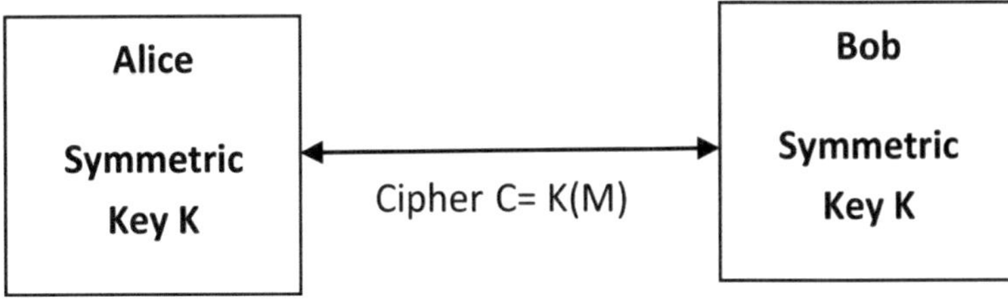

Figure 1. Symmetric-key cryptosystem.

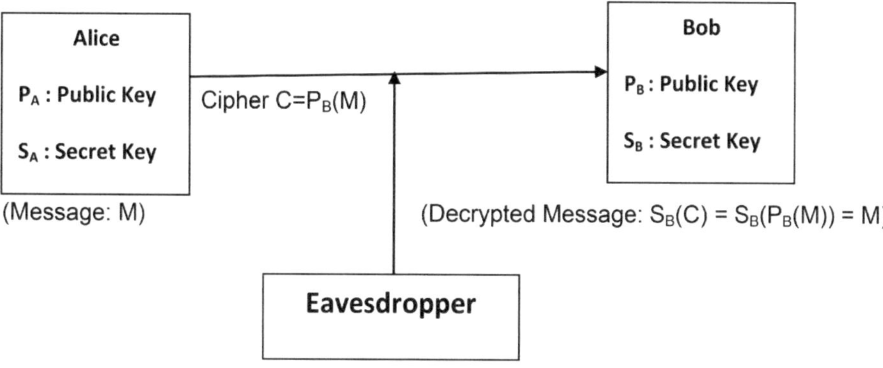

Figure 2. Public-key cryptosystem.

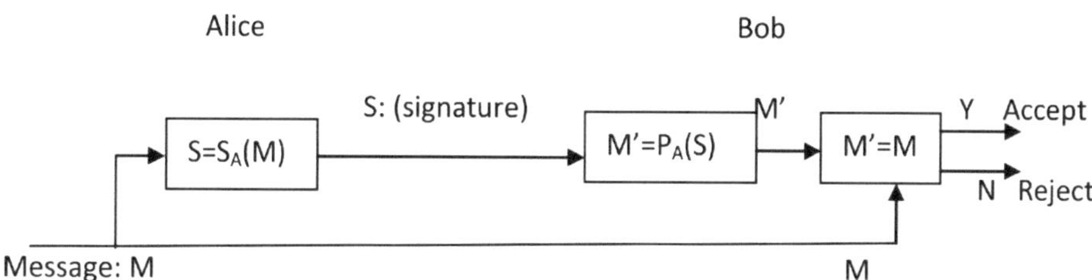

Figure 3. Authentication using digital signature.

Recently, we had seen the advent of IOT or Internet of Things. In a typical house, the household devices, such as television, fridge, microwave, washing machines, smoke detectors, etc. need to communicate with each other to relieve the end user from manual interventions in many real-time processes. Networking protocol TCP/IP was modified with RTP running over UDP for real-time applications. Over and above other issues of concern in this domination is limited computing, storage and energy, i.e., battery power. These devices usually use lightweight encryption/decryption algorithms since they are resource constrained. The major goal here is not to compromise the security and authenticity of the communicated data too much.

2. Conclusion

In the field of computers with the advent of Internet, the topic secure communication gained a significant importance. The theory of cryptography and coding theory evolved to handle many such problems. The emphases of these topics are both on secure communication that uses encryption and decryption schemes as well as on user authentication for the purpose of nonrepudiation. Subsequently, the topics of distributed and cloud computing emerged. Existing results related to cryptography and network security had to be tuned to adapt with these new technologies. More recently with the advancement of mobile technologies and Internet of Things (IOT), these algorithms had to take into consideration of limited resources like battery power, storage, and processor capabilities. This had led to the development of lightweight cryptography for resource-constrained devices. The topic of network security also had to face many challenges owing to variable interconnection topology instead of a fixed interconnection topology. For this reason the system becomes susceptible to various attacks from eavesdroppers. The book addresses these issues that arise in present day computing environments to overcome these security threats and also presents several possible directions for future research.

Author details

Pinaki Mitra

Address all correspondence to: pinaki@iitg.ac.in

Department of Computer Science and Engineering, IIT Guwahati, Guwahati, India

References

[1] Stallings W. Data and Computer Communications. Upper Saddle River, New Jersey: Pearson Education, Inc.; 2007

[2] Huffman DA. A method for the construction of minimum-redundancy codes. Proceedings of the IRE. 1952;**40**:1098-1101

[3] Welch T. A technique for high-performance data compression. Computer. 1984;**17**(6):8-19

[4] Ziv J, Lempel A. Compression of individual sequences via variable-rate coding. IEEE Transactions on Information Theory. 1978;**24**(5):530-536

[5] Stallings W. Cryptography and Network Security: Principles and Practice. Upper Saddle River, New Jersey: Prentice Hall, Inc.; 2005

Chapter 2

A New Approximation Method for Constant Weight Coding and Its Hardware Implementation

Jingwei Hu and Ray C.C. Cheung

Additional information is available at the end of the chapter

http://dx.doi.org/10.5772/intechopen.75041

Abstract

In this chapter, a more memory-efficient method for encoding binary information into words of prescribed length and weight is presented. The solutions in existing work include complex float point arithmetic or extra memory overhead which make it demanding for resource-constrained computing platform. The solution we propose here solves the problems above yet achieves better coding efficiency. We also correct a crucial error in previous implementations of code-based cryptography by exploiting and tweaking the proposed encoder. For the time being, the design presented in this work is the most compact one for any code-based encryption schemes. We show, for instance, that our lightweight implementation of Niederreiter encrypting unit can encrypt approximately 1 million plaintexts per second on a Xilinx Virtex-6 FPGA, requiring 183 slices and 18 memory blocks.

Keywords: code-based cryptography, McEliece/Niederreiter cryptosystem, constant weight coding, FPGA implementation

1. Introduction

Most modern public-key cryptographic systems rely on either the integer factorization or discrete logarithm problem, both of which expect to be solvable on large-scale quantum computers using Shor's algorithm [1]. The recent breakthroughs of powerful quantum computing have shown their strength in computing solutions to the hard mathematical problems mentioned [2, 3]. The cryptographic research community has identified the urgency of insecure vulnerabilities rooted in these cryptosystems and begun to settle their security on alternative hard problems in the last years, such as multivariate-quadratic, lattice-based, and code-based cryptosystems [4]. In this chapter, we address the problem of encoding information into binary

words of predefined length and Hamming weight in resource-constrained computing environment, e.g., reconfigurable hardware, embedded microcontroller systems, etc. This is of interest, in particular, of efficient implementations of McEliece's scheme [5, 6] or Niederreiter's scheme [7], the most prospective candidates for code-based cryptography.

In the case of Niederreiter/McEliece encryption, the binary stream of plaintext is requested to be converted into the form of constant weight words. Constant weight means that there exists a constant number of "1" in the binary plaintext. Note that in the hybrid Niederreiter encryption systems (KEM/DEM encryption) [8–10], KEMs are designed to exchange symmetric keys securely, and DEMs use these symmetric keys for transmitting long messages. This class of encryption techniques does not get constant weight coding involved. Nevertheless, if we want to construct a complete code-based cryptography including standard public-key encryption, digital signature, and hybrid encryption, constant weight coding must be efficiently implemented as it is required by both public-key encryption [11, 12] and signature [13]. The exact solution [14] of constant weight coding needs to compute large binomial coefficients and has a quadratic complexity though it is assumed to be optimal as a source coding algorithm. In [15], Sendrier proposed the first solution of linear complexity by incorporating Huffman codes. Later, the author of [15] further improves its coding efficiency very close to 1 by means of Goloumb's run-length encoding [16]. The new proposal is particularly easy to implement on hardware and has linear time complexity. The disadvantage though is that the length encoding is variable [17]. He also proposed an approximation version in this paper by regulating the value of d to the power of two. This approach significantly simplifies the encoding procedure and thus improves coding throughput.

Heyse et al. [18, 19] continued the research and proposed to adapt the approximation method in [17] to embedded system applications. Their design is implemented on AVR microcontrollers and Xilinx FPGAs. However, we observe that such method is not applicable to large parameter sets for the Niederreiter scheme (see **Table 1**) [20–22]. The work in [18, 19] preserves a lookup table of pre-stored data with the space complexity of $\mathcal{O}(n)$ to encode input messages into constant weight words. The memory overhead of this table is still intolerable for small embedded systems, and therefore their design is unscalable if n is large. CFS signature scheme [20] exploits very large Goppa code, and it requires to compress the lengthy constant weight signatures into a binary stream. MDPC-McEliece/Niederreiter encryption [23] uses very large n for practical security levels. For instance, n is set as large as 19,712 for 128-bit security and 65,536 for 256-bit security. Baldi et al. proposed a novel LDGM sparse syndrome signature scheme [13] with compact key size, which also requests a large constant weight coding within the signature generation. His method was successfully attacked in 2016 by a French research group [24]. At the time being, we do not have a considerably lightweight yet efficient solution for the constant weight encoding if we consider realizing such encoding in real-world applications.

The purpose of this work is to tweak Sendrier's approximation method [17] and hence to make it easy to implement for all possible secure parameters of the Niederreiter cryptosystem proposed in literature while maintaining the efficiency. Our contributions include:

1. We propose a new approximation method of constant weight coding free from complicated float point arithmetic and heavy memory footprint. This method permits us to implement a compact yet fast constant weight encoder on the resource-constrained computing platform.

(n, t)	Security level	Application	Coding system	Public/secret key size (kbits)	Prestored data for CW coding (kbits)
$(1024, 38)$	60 bit	Encryption	Goppa code	239/151.4	4
$(2048, 27)$	80 bit	Encryption	Goppa code	507/108.3	8
$(2690, 57)$	128 bit	Encryption	Goppa code	913/182.4	10.5
$(6624, 117)$	256 bit	Encryption	Goppa code	7488/2268.5	25.9
$(65536, 9)$	80 bit	Signature	Goppa code	9000/1019	256
$(262144, 9)$	80 bit	Signature	Goppa code	40,500/4525	1024
$(1048576, 8)$	80 bit	Signature	Goppa code	160,000/20,025	4096
$(9800, 18)$	80 bit	Signature	LDGM code	936/–	19.1
$(24960, 23)$	120 bit	Signature	LDGM code	4560/–	58.4
$(46000, 29)$	160 bit	Signature	LDGM code	13,480/–	117.2
$(19712, 134)$	128 bit	Encryption	MDPC code	9.6/–	77
$(65536, 264)$	256 bit	Encryption	MDPC code	32/–	256

Table 1. Parameters recommended used in the Niederreiter cryptosystem, referenced partly from [13, 19, 23, 25].

2. We improve the coding efficiency by fine-tuning the optimal precision for computing the value of *d*, in comparison with other approximation methods. The experiments have shown that the performance of our new method is better than Heyse's approximate version [18] and even comparable to Sendrier's original proposal [17].

3. We integrate our design with the Niederreiter encryption and obtain a more compact result. We fix a critical security flaw of Heyse et al.'s Niederreiter encryptor [19]. Our secure implementation of Niederreiter encryptor can encrypt approximately 1 million plaintexts per second on a Xilinx Virtex-6 FPGA, requiring 183 slices and 18 memory blocks.

This chapter is organized as follows. Sendrier's proposal of constant weight coding and its approximation variant [17, 18] is first revisited in Section 2. After analyzing the downside of these schemes, we are motivated to propose a new approximation method and to fine-tune it for an optimal source coding performance, presented in Section 3. Our detailed implementations for the proposed constant weight encoder/decoder and Niederreiter encryption unit on FPGAs are described in Section 4 and Section 5. We present our experimental results compared with the state of arts in Section 6. Finally, Section 7 summarizes this chapter.

2. Sendrier's methods for constant weight coding

Sendrier presented an algorithm for encoding binary information into words of prescribed length and weight [17]. His encoding algorithm returns a *t*-tuple $(\delta_1, \delta_2, \ldots, \delta_t)$ in which δ_i s are the lengths of the longest strings of consecutive "0"s. This method is easy to implement and has linear complexity with a small loss of information efficiency. In this work, we unfold the recursive encoding and decoding algorithms originated from [17] and rewrite them in Algorithm 1 and Algorithm 2 [26].

Algorithm 1: Encode Binary String to Constant Weight Word (Bin2CW) [26]

```
Input: message length n, message weight t and a binary stream B
Output: a t-tuple Δ = (δ_1, δ_2, ..., δ_t)
δ = 0, index = 1
while t > 0 do
    if n ≤ t then
        t−−, n−−
        δ_index = δ
        δ = 0, index++
    else
        d = best_d(n, t)
        if read(B, 1) = 1 then
            n −= d, δ += d
        else
            i = decodefd(d, B)
            δ_index = δ + i
            n −= (i + 1), t−−, δ = 0, index++
return (δ_1, ..., δ_t)
```

Algorithm 2: Decode Constant Weight Word to Binary String (CW2Bin) [26]

```
Input: n, t and a t-tuple Δ = (δ_1, δ_2, ..., δ_t)
Output: a binary string B
index = 1
while t != 0 and n > t do
    d = best_d(n, t)
    if δ_index ≥ d then
        n −= d, δ_index −= d
        write(B, 1)
    else
        write(B, 0)
        write(B, encodefd(δ_index, d))
        n −= (δ_index + 1), t−−, index++
return B
```

We use the same notations from [17, 26] in the above two algorithms to keep consistency. For example, read(B, i) moves forward and reads i bits in the stream B and returns the integer whose binary decomposition has been read, most significant bit first; Write(B, i) moves forward and writes the binary string i into the stream B; and encodefd(δ_{index}, d) returns a binary string and decodefd(d, B) returns an integer. These two functions are actually the run-length encoding and decoding methods proposed by Golomb [16, 17]. best_d(n, t) returns an integer such that $1 \leq$best_d$(n, t) \leq n - t$ and Sendrier suggested to choose it close to the number defined by Eq. (1). In fact, best_d(n, t) can take any value in the range though the efficiency would be reduced if this value is too far from Eq. (1):

$$d = \left(n - \frac{t-1}{2}\right)\left(1 - \frac{1}{2^{\frac{1}{t}}}\right) \tag{1}$$

Sendrier also presented an approximation of the best d where the values of d (given by Eq. (1)) was restricted to the power of two [17]. More precisely, d is first computed via Eq. (1) and then round to $2^{\lceil \log_2(d) \rceil}$. This approximation greatly simplifies the functions of encodefd$(\cdot)$ and decodefd$(\cdot)$ and therefore outperforms in speed, while the loss of coding efficiency is trivial. The simplified versions of encoding and decoding with encodefd$(\cdot)$ and decodefd$(\cdot)$ after approximation are described as follows [26]:

$$\text{encodefd}(\delta, d) = base_2(\delta, u) \tag{2}$$

$$\text{decodefd}(d, B) = read(B, u) \tag{3}$$

where $base_2(\delta, u)$ denotes the u least significant bits of the integer δ written in base 2 and $u = \lceil \log_2(d) \rceil$. For the above two equations, the minimum allowed value of d is noteworthy in the case of $d = 1$. In this case we have $u = 0$, and therefore we define by purpose that $base_2(\delta, 0) = null$ and $read(B, 0) = 0$ to guarantee that our algorithm applies to all possible u.

Recently, Heyse et al. implemented Niederreiter encryption scheme on embedded microcontrollers in which they used a lookup table to compute the value of d for constant weight encoding [18]. Their method is based on the approximation method from [17]. One major contribution of their work is they observe that the last few bits of n can be ignored for constant weight encoding because these bits make little difference to the value of d. They do not keep $n \cdot t$ entries but instead n entries; the least significant $\lceil \log_2 t \rceil$ bits of n are not considered and are substituted by t. This method significantly reduces the size of the lookup table. According to our analysis, the lookup table is shrunk to roughly $\mathcal{O}(n)$. It works pretty well for small parameters of n, for example, $n = 2^{11}$ in the applications of Goppa code-based McEliece or Niederreiter encryption schemes. However, we occasionally found that it does not work well when we were implementing a Niederreiter signature scheme, called CFS signature. CFS requires an extremely large value of n, typically $n = 2^{18}, n = 2^{20}$. On the one hand, the size of lookup table increases linearly with n, resulting in somewhat unscalability. On the other hand, the coding efficiency drops dramatically and thus lowers the throughput of the constant weight encoder as n increases. All these downsides motivate us to figure out better ways of computing d. We would describe and analyze our new methods in the next section.

3. Proposed approximation method of *d*

3.1. Reduce memory footprint and computational steps

The computation of the value of d is the most crucial step of constant weight encoding and decoding, as suggested by Eq. (1) which involves floating-point arithmetic. However, many embedded/hardware systems do not have dedicated floating-point units for such computations.

[19] proposed to replace floating-point units by a lookup table with predefined data for reconfigurable hardware. The problem of their method is that, for some large (n, t), the lookup table could be sizeable. For example, $(n = 2^{16}, t = 9)$ requests the size of lookup table to be 256 kb, which is obviously not a negligible memory overhead for embedded systems.

To solve this problem, we propose to eliminate such lookup table by computing d directly using fixed-point arithmetic. We separate the computation of d into two parts. In the first part, $\theta[t] = \left(1 - 1/2^{\frac{1}{t}}\right)$ is precomputed and stored in the fixed-point format. In the second part, $\left(n - \frac{t-1}{2}\right) \cdot \theta$ is then efficiently calculated by a fixed-point multiplier. In this fashion we notably shrink the size of lookup table from $\mathcal{O}(n)$ to $\mathcal{O}(t)$ [26].

Furthermore, we substitute $\left(n - \frac{t-1}{2}\right)$ by n due to the following observations [26]:

- $n \gg t$ such that $n - \frac{t-1}{2} \approx n$.
- Eventually d must be round to an integer, and hence the difference between $\left(n - \frac{t-1}{2}\right)\theta$ and $n\theta$ is very likely to be ignored.

This substitution enables the removal of the computational steps of $n - (t-1)/2$, and hence a faster and simpler realization of constant coding which makes use of a single integer multiplication is achievable.

In summary, our new proposal of the approximation of d is as follows [26]:

$$d = \lfloor n \cdot \theta[t] \rfloor \tag{4}$$

where $\theta[t] = \left(1 - 1/2^{\frac{1}{t}}\right)$ is a function of t and precomputed. Our new approximation of d is lightweight, requiring only one multiplication. In the following, we will demonstrate that this method also permits reasonable high-coding efficiency as a source coding algorithm.

3.2. Represent $\theta[t]$ in fixed-point format

As aforementioned, $\theta[t]$ is actually a vector of fractional numbers and should be stored in fixed-point format. Note that the integer part of $\theta[t]$ is always 0, and therefore we only need to preserve its fractional part. Hereafter, we denote our fixed-point format as fixed_0_i, where i indicates the bits we have used for storing the fractional part of $\theta[t]$.

In practice, we hope to use fixed_0_i with the smallest i while maintaining desirable coding efficiency [26]. Smaller i means lower data storage and a simpler multiplication with smaller operand size, which is particularly advisable for resource-constrained computing platforms. Indeed, one of the key issues of this chapter is to determine the best fixed_0_i for $\theta[t]$. In the next section, we describe our experiments on exploring the optimal fixed_0_i.

3.3. Find the optimal precision for constant weight encoding

The purpose of the precision tuning is to find the lowest precision that still maintains a relatively high coding efficiency. A lower precision means we can use a multiplier of smaller operand size leading to better path delay and slice utilization. A higher coding efficiency means one can encode more bits from the source into a constant weight word. This is of interest, in particular, when someone encrypts a relatively large file using code-based crypto: It takes much less time for encryption if we have a high coding efficiency close to 1 [26].

To find the optimal precision of fixed_0_i, we studied the relationship between distinct i's and their coding performance. In our experiments, all possible precision from fp_0_32 to fp_0_1 are investigated to compare with the Sendrier's methods [17] and Heyse's approximate version [18].

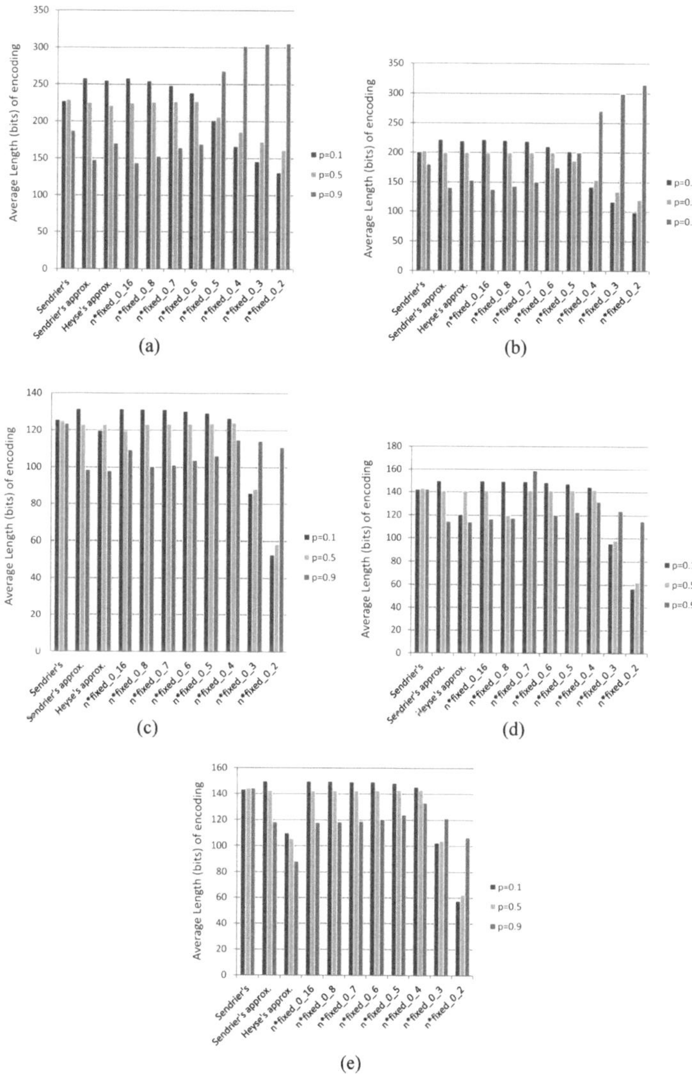

Figure 1. The performance of different methods for choosing the optimal d. We have listed five most frequently used sets of (n, t) for the Niederreiter cryptosystem. We have done three experiments for each (n, t) in which the input binary message contains "1" with the probability $p = 0.1$, 0.5, and 0.9, respectively. The results of each experiment are obtained by running 10,000 different messages. The X-axis lists different methods including Senderier's primitive [17], Senderier's approximation [17], Heyse's approximation [19], and our n*fixed_0_16 − N*fixed_0_2. The Y-axis represents the average length (bits) of the input message read for a successful constant weight encoding.

We measured the coding efficiency by calculating the average coding length for a successful encoding because longer coding length indicates a better coding efficiency. Since constant weight coding is variable length coding, we must consider how different plaintexts as input could affect the performance in order to determine which approximation is the best. To be thorough, different types of binary plaintexts, classified by the proportion of "1" contained, should be tested for evaluating the real performance of different encoding approximation methods. In our instances, we measure three particular types to simplify the model: "0" dominated texts (p = 0.1, "1" exists with probability of 0.1 in the plaintext), balanced texts (p = 0.5, "1" exists with probability of 0.5), and "1" dominated texts (p = 0.9, "1" exists with probability of 0.9) (**Figure 1**).

Figure 2 describes the coding performances when we adjust the precision of $\theta[t]$. Taken as a whole, the p = 0.1 group and the p = 0.5 group have a similar trend of average message length encoded as the arithmetic precision decreases: The message length drops slightly from n*fixed_0_16 — n*fixed_0_2 in consistency. On the contrary, the p = 0.9 group appears to be quite different where the numbers of bits read for a single constant weight coding first stay stable and

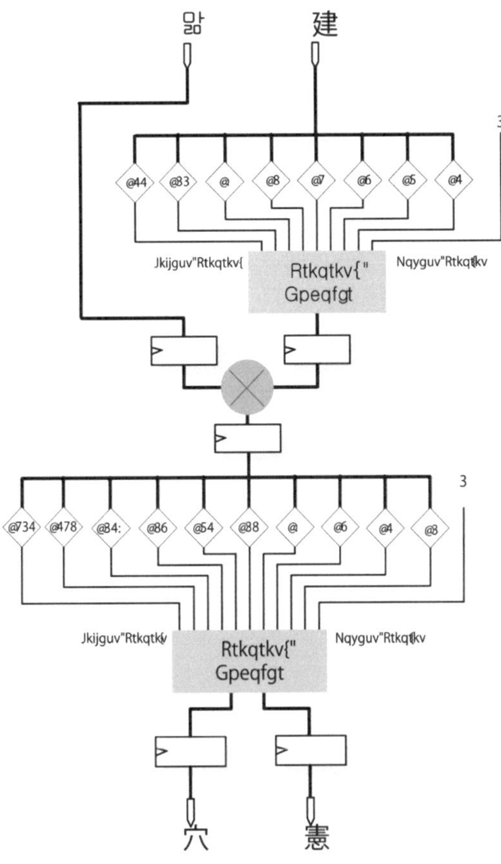

Figure 2. best_d module for CW encoder and decoder. We list here the detailed configurations of $n = 2^{11}, t = 27$ for demonstrative purpose.

then drop with the approximation precision decreasing. The numbers first keep stable because the loss of precision in $\theta[t]$ is comparatively trivial but if the precision drops too low, for instance, with fixed_0_2 representation $\theta[t] = 0$ for $2 \le t \le 38$ and hence $d = 0$. It leads to a constant n and small value of i in Algorithm 3 forcing us to read more bits of input stream before the algorithm halts. According to the evaluation criteria mentioned in the last paragraph, we compute the average length of the three types of plaintexts and identify the best approximation of d from our proposal after analyzing the statistics obtained. On the one hand, the n*fixed_0_5 group outperforms at $(n = 2^{10}, t = 38)$ and $(n = 2^{11}, t = 27)$. On the other hand, the n*fixed_0_4 group beats the others at $(n = 2^{16}, t = 9)$, $(n = 2^{18}, t = 9)$, and $(n = 2^{20}, t = 8)$.

Table 2 compares our proposed methods with the Sendrier's [17], Sendrier's original approximation using power of 2 [17], and Heyse's table lookup approximation [18]. From this table, it is seen that our proposal gains better coding efficiency than the original approximation and Heyse's approximation among all five parameter sets used for the Niederreiter scheme. Note that the average number of bits we have to read before producing the constant weight words is

n	t	Method	Number of bits read			Coding efficiency	Efficiency improved
			Maximum	Minimum	Average		
2^{10}	38	Sendrier's [17]	236	164	214.70	93.19%	—
		Sendrier's approx. [17]	263	124	210.45	91.32%	−1.98%
		Heyse's approx. [19]	261	143	210.73	91.44%	−1.85%
		n*fixed_0_5	311	183	225.54	97.89%	**+5.05%**
2^{11}	27	Sendrier's [17]	208	160	194.46	95.51%	—
		Sendrier's approx. [17]	227	119	187.55	92.11%	−3.56%
		Heyse's approx. [19]	224	127	190.96	93.78%	−1.80%
		n*fixed_0_5	361	132	196.30	96.41%	**+0.95%**
2^{16}	9	Sendrier's [17]	133	113	124.87	99.50%	—
		Sendrier's approx. [17]	133	77	117.80	93.84%	−5.10%
		Heyse's approx. [19]	133	86	116.34	92.68%	−6.83%
		n*fixed_0_4	135	95	121.98	97.20%	**−2.37%**
2^{18}	9	Sendrier's [17]	148	132	142.61	99.38%	—
		Sendrier's approx. [17]	151	91	135.17	94.18%	−5.22%
		Heyse's approx. [19]	300	101	133.21	92.81%	−6.60%
		n*fixed_0_4	154	112	139.64	97.31%	**−2.08%**
2^{20}	8	Sendrier's [17]	149	135	144.00	99.52%	—
		Sendrier's approx. [17]	151	99	136.94	94.64%	−4.90%
		Heyse's approx. [19]	265	17	110.07	76.07%	−23.56%
		n*fixed_0_4	158	109	140.81	97.31%	**−2.22%**

Table 2. The coding performance of the optimal d chosen from our approximation method.

upper bound by $\log_2\binom{n}{t}$, and the thus the ratio of the average number read and the upper bound measures the coding efficiency [17]. Additionally, our proposal even outperforms the Sendrier's method at two of these parameter sets— $(n = 2^{10}, t = 38)$ and $(n = 2^{11}, t = 27)$ with 5.05 and 0.95% of improvements, respectively. It is also worth mentioning that for $(n = 2^{16}, t = 9)$, $(n = 2^{18}, t = 9)$, and $(n = 2^{20}, t = 8)$, the performance of our proposal falls slightly behind with 2.37, 2.08, and 2.22% of loss when compared with the Sendrier's method; it nonetheless outruns Sendrier's approximation and Heyse's approximation. In particular, the performance of Heyse's approximation becomes unfavorable with 23.56% loss at $(n = 2^{20}, t = 8)$, and we are pushing the limits of Heyse's method here as the lower bits of n are innegligible and cannot be removed with such large n.

4. Proposed constant weight encoder and decoder

4.1. best_d module

The best_d module is the most critical arithmetic unit which computes the best value of d according to the inputs n and t. Our proposal of computation of *best_d* consists of three stages which performs the following task in sequence:

1. **Compute $\theta[t]$ via a priority encoder.** As discussed in Section 3, format fixed_0_5 is chosen to represent $\theta[t]$ for $(n = 2^{10}, t = 38)$ and $(n = 2^{11}, t = 27)$, and fixed_0_4 is used for

Value of t	$\theta[t] = (0.\theta_1\theta_2\theta_3\theta_4\theta_5)_2$ *	$\theta[t] = (0.\theta_1\theta_2\theta_3\theta_4)_2$ †
$22 \le t \le 38$	00000	N/A
$11 \le t \le 21$	00001	
$8 \le t \le 10$	00010	0001
$6 \le t \le 7$	00011	
$t = 5$	00100	0010
$t = 4$	00101	
$t = 3$	00110	0011
$t = 2$	01001	0100
$t = 1$	10,000	1000

*This $\theta[t]$ is represented in fixed_0_5 form, e.g., $\theta[t] = \sum_{i=1}^{5} \theta_i \cdot 2^{-i}$. This format is used in $(n = 2^{10}, t = 38)$ and $(n = 2^{11}, t = 27)$.

†This $\theta[t]$ is represented in fixed_0_4 form, e.g., $\theta[t] = \sum_{i=1}^{4} \theta_i \cdot 2^{-i}$. This format is used in $(n = 2^{16}, t = 9)$, $(n = 2^{18}, t = 9)$, and $(n = 2^{20}, t = 8)$.

Table 3. Encoding of $\theta[t]$.

$(n = 2^{16}, t = 9)$, $n = 2^{18}, t = 9$, and $n = 2^{20}, t = 8$. We notice via analysis that for some t, the values of $\theta[t]$ are identical. For instance, $\theta[6] = \theta[7] = (0.00011)_2 = 0.09375$ in fixed_0_5 format, shown in **Table 3**. This observation inspires us to exploit priority encoder to streamline the encoding of $\theta[t]$.

2. **Compute $n \cdot \theta[t]$ via a fixed-point multiplier.** Xilinx LogiCORE IP is configured to implement high-performance, optimized multipliers for different pairs of n and t. The fractional part of the multiplication result is truncated, but its integer part is preserved for the next stage to process.

3. **Output the value of d and u.** Recall that the value of $n \cdot \theta[t]$ must be round to $d = 2^u$. Another priority encoder is utilized to decode the integer part of $n \cdot \theta[t]$. The detailed decoding process is structured as lookup table mapping illustrated in **Table 4**.

Integer part of $n \cdot \theta[t]$	Value of d	Value of u
$n\theta[t] > 2^{18}$	2^{19}	19
$2^{17} < n\theta[t] \le 2^{18}$	2^{18}	18
$2^{16} < n\theta[t] \le 2^{17}$	2^{17}	17
$2^{15} < n\theta[t] \le 2^{16}$	2^{16}	16
$2^{14} < n\theta[t] \le 2^{15}$	2^{15}	15
$2^{13} < n\theta[t] \le 2^{14}$	2^{14}	14
$2^{12} < n\theta[t] \le 2^{13}$	2^{13}	13
$2^{11} < n\theta[t] \le 2^{12}$	2^{12}	12
$2^{10} < n\theta[t] \le 2^{11}$	2^{11}	11
$2^{9} < n\theta[t] \le 2^{10}$	2^{10}	10
$2^{8} < n\theta[t] \le 2^{9}$	2^{9}	9
$2^{7} < n\theta[t] \le 2^{8}$	2^{8}	8
$2^{6} < n\theta[t] \le 2^{7}$	2^{7}	7
$2^{5} < n\theta[t] \le 2^{6}$	2^{6}	6
$2^{4} < n\theta[t] \le 2^{5}$	2^{5}	5
$2^{3} < n\theta[t] \le 2^{4}$	2^{4}	4
$2^{2} < n\theta[t] \le 2^{3}$	2^{3}	3
$2 < n\theta[t] \le 2^{2}$	2^{2}	2
$1 < n\theta[t] \le 2$	2	1
$n\theta[t] \le 1$	1	0

Table 4. Decoding of $n \cdot \theta[t]$.

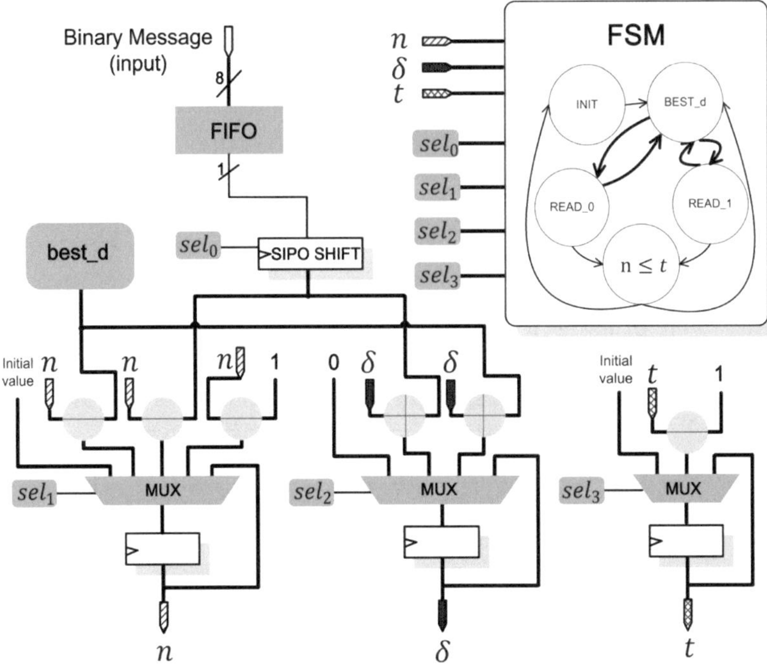

Figure 3. General architecture of CW encoder.

Figure 2 depicts our best_d unit. This unit works in three-stage pipelines. It first computes $\theta[t]$ and then obtains $n \cdot \theta[t]$ using a multiplier. Finally, the value of d would be determined by a priority decoder.

4.2. Bin2CW encoder

Figure 3 overviews the architecture of the proposed constant weight encoder. Input binary message is passed inward the encoder by means of nonsymmetric 8-to-1 FIFO-read which exactly imitates the function of $\text{read}(B, 1)$. A serial-in-parallel-out shift register is instantiated to perform $\text{read}(B, u), 0 \leq u \leq \left\lceil \log_2 \binom{n}{2} \right\rceil$. The proposed best_d module is exploited here to calculate the value of d. The values of n, t, and δ are accordingly refreshed using three separate registers.

4.3. CW2Bin decoder

Figure 4 renders the architecture of the proposed constant weight decoder. A symmetric m-to-m bit FIFO is used to read the input t-tuple word by word. This logic is indeed the bottleneck of the constant weight decoder when compared with the encoder. Three registers are utilized to update the values of n and t as the Bin2CW encoder does, δ. The major difference is that the shift register here outputs the value of δ bit by bit as step 9 of Algorithm 2 demands.

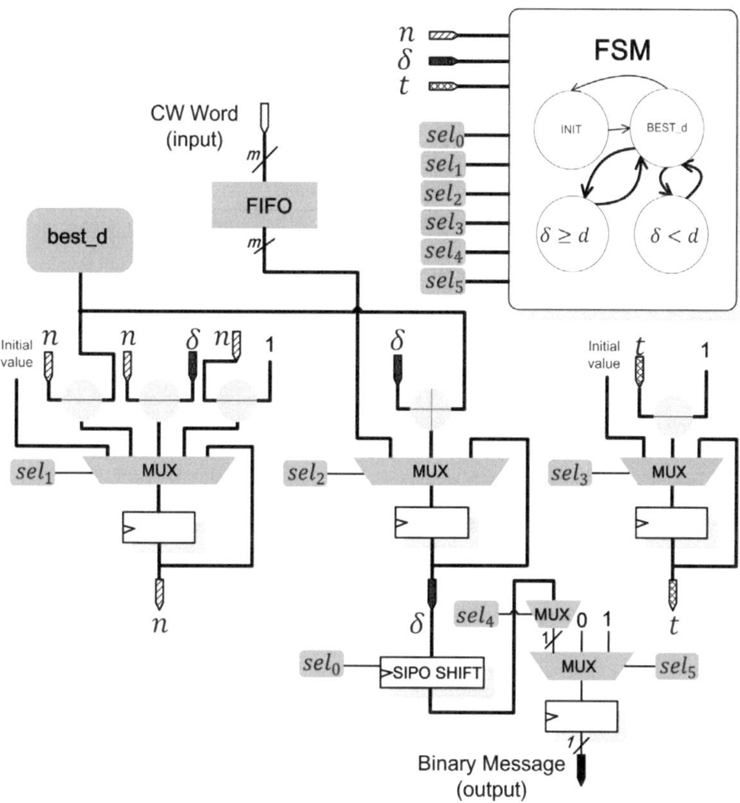

Figure 4. General architecture of CW decoder.

5. Integrating with the Niederreiter encryptor

In this section, we demonstrate that the proposed Bin2CW encoder can integrate into the Niederreiter encryptor for data encryption, shown in Algorithm 3.

Algorithm 3. Niederreiter Message Encryption, referenced from [25]

Input: message vector m, public key $pk = \{\widehat{H}, t\}$ where $\widehat{H}$ is an n by mt matrix

Output: ciphertext c

1 Bob encodes the message m as a binary matrix/vector of length n and weight at most t.

2 Bob computes the ciphertext as $c = \widehat{H}m^T$; m^T is the transpose of matrix m.

3 **return** c.

The Bin2CW encoder performs the first step in Algorithm 3. Note that Bin2CW encoder returns a t-tuple of integers $(\delta_1, \ldots, \delta_t)$, which represents the distance between consecutive "1"s in the string. Nevertheless such t-tuple cannot be directly transported to compute the ciphertext. We believe that the way Heyse et al. [19] encrypts $c = \widehat{H}m^T$ with $m = (\delta_1, \ldots, \delta_t)$ is incorrect due to two reasons [26]:

1. It is very likely that $\delta_i = \delta_j$ where $i \neq j$ such that the number of errors is less than t, and it is assumed to be insecure for cryptanalysis.
2. $(\delta_1, \ldots, \delta_t)$ returns the integer ranging from 0 to $n - t$, but the constant weight word exactly ranges from 0 to n. In other terms, the last t rows of the public key $\widehat{H}^T$ are never used.

To correct this weakness from [19], we propose to generate the "real" constant weight binary words of length n and Hamming weight t. Assume the constant weight is represented by $(i_1, \ldots, i_t)$, the coordinates of the "1"s in ascending order, then $i_1 = \delta_1$, $i_2 = \delta_2 + i_1 + 1$, …, and $i_t = \delta_t + i_{t-1} + 1$ are computed as the input of the second step, Algorithm 3.

Figure 5 illustrates our revision of Niederreiter encryption unit on the basis of [19]. The public key $\widehat{H}^T$ is stored in an internal BRAM and row-wise addressed by the 11-bit register. Two 11-bit integer adders are instantiated to transform $(\delta_1, \ldots, \delta_t)$ to $(i_1, \ldots, i_t)$ which are eventually stored in the 11-bit register. The vector–matrix multiplication in step 2, Algorithm 3, is equivalent to XOR operation of the selected rows of $\widehat{H}^T$, which can be implemented as a $GF(2^{297})$ adder in this figure. It is also worth noting that the vector–matrix multiplication works concurrently with the CW encoding: Whenever a valid i_k has been computed, it is transferred immediately to the $GF(2^{297})$ adder for summing up the selected row. Once the last i_t has been

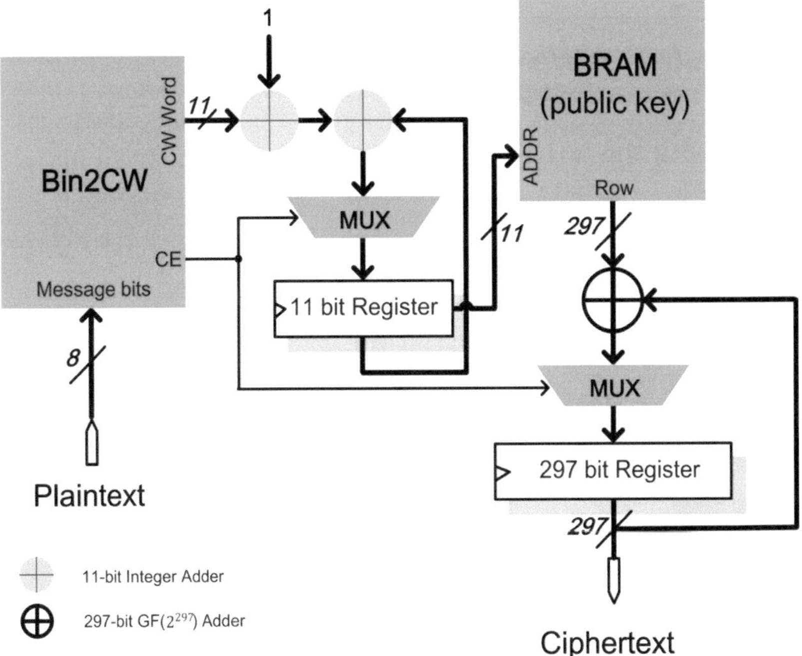

Figure 5. Block diagram of the Niederreiter encryptor.

computed, the last indexed row of $\widehat{H}^T$ also has been accumulated to the sum. This sum, stored in the 297-bit register, is now available to be interpreted as the ciphertext.

Our final remark is for the side channel attacks of code-based crypto using constant weight encoding (CWE). Admittedly, we cannot give a satisfying answer of them at the time being. We believe this is an open problem left to be solved. For the time being, if the users decide not to take the risk of timing attacks, we suggest forcing the CWE to be constant time. We can set the maximum time (it happens when we have all-zero input) for whatever the input is. Nevertheless, the price is a significant drop of timing performance.

We give here our analysis of timing attacks: The attackers can compromise the CWE if and only if he could analyze the timing differences among different inputs and use this information to recover the entire message. Unfortunately, the timing character of the operation of reading "1" or "0" is different: when reading "1," it consumes only 1 clock cycle count, whereas when reading "1," it continues to read $\lceil \log_2(d) \rceil$ more bits from B, consuming $1 + \lceil \log_2(d) \rceil$ counts. These behaviors appear at first sight to be vulnerable to timing attacks: For different inputs, the execution time is slightly different, and the distinction between reading "0" and reading "1" is also significant. However, statistical approaches as [27, 28] have introduced against RSA cryptosystems which seem to be not helpful: To our way of thinking, the situation we encounter is much more difficult. (1) We need to recover this particular message under attack, but the timing differences among different messages that we collect do not leak any useful information on the targeted message. On the contrary, in RSA we can use a large number of messages and compare the timing for recovering the secret key in a bit-by-bit fashion. (2) Note that d is changing each iteration according to the current state of n and t. That is to say, when reading "1," the timing is variable, sensitive to how "1" and "0" are permuted in the message and thus difficult to predict. Most importantly, even if CWE is somehow compromised, it does not reveal any information about secret keys. In the case of decryption, the ciphertext is first decrypted by an error correcting decoder (typically, Goppa-code or MDPC-code decoder) which holds the secret key. The result after error correcting is a $GF(2^n)$ vector, and then this vector is encoded by CWE for the plaintext recovered. We can see the key points here: Timing attacks should be mounted on error correcting decoders rather than constant weight decoders for retrieving the secret keys. Perhaps a better strategy is to mount timing attacks on CWE for recovering the plaintext directly. This raises one more question: how do we distinguish or measure the peculiar timing of CWE out of the total execution time, given that error correcting decoders also take nonconstant time for decoding? This is indeed a very exciting topic for which we would investigate in our future work.

6. Results and comparisons

We captured our constant weight coding architecture in the Verilog language and prototyped our design on Xilinx Virtex-6 FPGA (**Table 5**). The reason why we did our experiments on Xilinx Virtex-6 is principally about a convention. Recent progress in FPGA implementations of

	Algorithm	Platform	Area [slices]	Memory blocks [36 + 18 kb RAM]	Frequency [MHz]	Throughout [Mbps]	Coding efficiency
(a) $n = 2^{10}$, $t = 38$							
This work	Bin2CW, new approx.	Xilinx xc6vlx240t	74	0 + 1	330	160.2	97.89%
	CW2Bin, new approx.		79	0 + 1	330	148.1	
Heyse et al. [19]	Bin2CW, Heyse's approx.	Xilinx xc6vlx240t	110	0 + 1	310	178.8	91.44%
	CW2Bin, Heyse's approx.		88	0 + 1	310	162.1	
(b) $n = 2^{11}$, $t = 27$							
This work	Bin2CW, new approx.	Xilinx xc6vlx240t	91	0 + 1	350	187.2	96.41%
	CW2Bin, new approx.		95	0 + 1	340	168.6	
Heyse et al. [19]	Bin2CW, Heyse's approx.	Xilinx xc6vlx240t	118	0 + 1	340	208.4	93.78%
	CW2Bin, Heyse's approx.		110	0 + 1	340	164.6	
Sendrier [17]*	Bin2CW, original	Intel Pentium 4	—	—	2400	17.3	95.51%
	Bin2CW, approximate					33.0	92.11%
(c) $n = 2^{16}$, $t = 9$							
This work	Bin2CW, new approx.	Xilinx xc6vlx240t	103	0 + 1	440	316.1	97.20%
	CW2Bin, new approx.		109	0 + 1	310	212.9	
Heyse et al. [19]	Bin2CW, Heyse's approx.	Xilinx xc6vlx240t	90	10 + 3	240	182.3	92.68%
	CW2Bin, Heyse's approx.		90	10 + 3	230	170.3	
Sendrier [17]	Bin2CW, original	Intel Pentium 4	—	—	2400	18.3	99.50%
	Bin2CW, approximate					22.0	93.84%
(d) $n = 2^{18}$, $t = 9$							
This work	Bin2CW, new approx.	Xilinx xc6vlx240t	138	0 + 1	410	295.5	97.31%
	CW2Bin, new approx.		118	0 + 1	320	219.5	
Heyse et al. [19]	Bin2CW, Heyse's approx.	Xilinx xc6vlx240t	94	40 + 3	170	106.0	92.81%
	CW2Bin, Heyse's approx.		93	40 + 3	180	104.9	

	Algorithm	Platform	Area [slices]	Memory blocks [36 + 18 kb RAM]	Frequency [MHz]	Throughout [Mbps]	Coding efficiency
(e) $n = 2^{20}$, $t = 8$							
This work	Bin2CW, new approx.	Xilinx xc6vlx240t	156	0 + 1	370	284.9	97.31%
	CW2Bin, new approx.		122	0 + 1	300	222.7	
Heyse et al. [19]	Bin2CW, Heyse's approx.	Xilinx xc6vlx240t	124	160 + 3	130	96.6	76.07%
	CW2Bin, Heyse's approx.		125	160 + 3	130	98.8	

*Sendrier implemented a different but very close parameter set $n = 2^{11}$, $t = 30$. We also put it here for reference.

Table 5. Compact implementations of CW encoder and decoder on Xilinx Virtex-6 FPGA.

code-based cryptography accept Virtex-6 or even lower ends for implementation aspects [19, 29–32]. The benefit of using Virtex-6 from our standpoint is that we could fairly compare our design with others given that most of them are also implemented on Virtex-6. To the best of our knowledge, the only compact implementations of constant weight coding have been proposed by Heyse et al. [19]. Their lightweight architecture is generally identical to ours except the design of best_d module. Their best_d module works in two pipeline stages: In the first stage, it retrieves the value of u by table lookup. Then in the second stage, it outputs d according to the value of u using a simple decoder. Comparatively, our best_d module has three stages of the pipeline, and thus it leads to a lower throughput, but our architectures are smaller and improve the area-time tradeoff of the constant weight coding implementations proposed by Heyse et al. [19], shown in **Table 5**. In particular, we use only one 18 kb memory block for all parameter sets of our experiments.

We also observe that in our designs, the memory footprint does not increase, and the high clock frequency also maintains as the parameters grow. This is because the main difference among encoders or decoders with distinct parameters n and t is the data width of multiplier embedded in the best_d module, which increases logarithmically from $10bit \times 5bit$ to $20bit \times 4bit$. On the other hand, the memory overhead of Heyse's implementations grows linearly with n and might introduce problems when n is large as aforementioned. To verify this argument, we re-implemented Heyse's work for $\left(n = 2^{16}, t = 9\right)$, $\left(n = 2^{18}, t = 9\right)$, and $\left(n = 2^{20}, t = 8\right)$. The experimental results validate this point. Additionally, another negative side effect of heavy memory overhead is that the working frequency of circuits drops rapidly as shown in **Table 6**. For small parameters (a) and (b), the lookup table in Heyse's design could be made of distributed memory (LUT) and therefore has little impact on frequency. However, for large parameters (c), (d), and (e), such lookup table can no longer be instantiated as LUTs because Xilinx Virtex-6 distributed memory generator only allows maximum data depth of 6,5536. We instead use block memory resource of the FPGAs to construct the table, and this accordingly hinders speed performance due to relatively far and complicated routing. The usage of block memory is the real bottleneck of Heyse's work as n grows.

Aspect (Virtex6-VLX240)	Niederreiter [12]	This work
Slices	315	183
LUTs	926	505
FFs	875	498
BRAMs	17	18*
Frequency	300 MHz	340 MHz
CW encode $e = \text{Bin2CW}(m)$	≈200 cycles	349.1 cycles
Encrypt $c = e \cdot \widehat{H}$	≈200 cycles	352.1 cycles

*We used 16×36kb RAMs and 2×16kb RAMs.

Table 6. FPGA implementation results of Niederreiter encryption with $n = 2048, t = 27$ compared with [19] after PAR.

We finally implemented the Niederreiter encryptor, a cryptographic application where constant weight coding is used exactly as described in Section 5. **Table 6** compares our work with the state of art [19, 26]. It is seen that our new implementation is the most compact, with better area-time tradeoffs. The same amount of block memory is occupied in our design as [19] did where 16 × 36kb + 1 × 18kb RAMs are utilized to save the public-key matrix $\widehat{H}$ and one 18 kb RAM for the 8-to-1 FIFO within the constant weight encoder.

7. Conclusion

A new approach for determining the optimal value d in constant weight coding is proposed in this chapter. This method innovates a more compact yet efficient architecture for constant weight encoder and decoder in resource-constrained computing systems. Afterward, we exploited this new encoder to implement the Niederreiter encryptor on a Xilinx device. Experiments show that our work competes for the state of art and works better in terms of both RAM usage and processing throughput for large parameters.

Author details

Jingwei Hu* and Ray C.C. Cheung

*Address all correspondence to: jw.hu@cityu.edu.hk

Department of Electronic Engineering, City University of Hong Kong, Hong Kong

References

[1] Shor PW. Polynomial-time algorithms for prime factorization and discrete logarithms on a quantum computer. SIAM Journal on Computing. 1997;**26**(5):1484-1509

[2] Vandersypen LM, Steffen M, Breyta G, Yannoni CS, Sherwood MH, Chuang IL. Experimental realization of Shor's quantum factoring algorithm using nuclear magnetic resonance. Nature. 2001;**414**(6866):883-887

[3] Xu N, Zhu J, Lu D, Zhou X, Peng X, Du J. Quantum factorization of 143 on a dipolar-coupling nmr system. arXiv preprint arXiv:1111.3726; 2011

[4] Bernstein DJ. Introduction to post-quantum cryptography. In: Post-Quantum Cryptography. Berlin: Springer; 2009. pp. 1-14

[5] McEliece RJ. A public-key cryptosystem based on algebraic coding theory. DSN Progress Report. 1978;**42**(44):114-116

[6] Sendrier N. Code-based public-key cryptography. In: Post-Quantum Cryptography Summer School. 2014

[7] Niederreiter H. Knapsack-type cryptosystems and algebraic coding theory. Problems Of Control and Information Theory-Problemy Upravleniya I Thorii Informatsii. 1986;**15**(2): 159-166

[8] Persichetti E. Secure and anonymous hybrid encryption from coding theory. In: International Workshop on Post-Quantum Cryptography. Springer; 2013. pp. 174-187

[9] von Maurich I, Heberle L, Güneysu T. Ind-cca secure hybrid encryption from qc-mdpc niederreiter. In: International Workshop on Post-Quantum Cryptography; Springer; 2016. pp. 1-17

[10] Chou T. Qcbits: Fast constant-time code-based cryptography. In: Cryptographic Hardware and Embedded Systems-CHES 2016; Springer. 2016. pp. 250-272

[11] Biswas B, Sendrier N. Mceliece cryptosystem implementation: Theory and practice. In: International Workshop on Post-Quantum Cryptography; Springer; 2008. pp. 47-62

[12] Overbeck R, Sendrier N. Code-based cryptography. In: Post-Quantum Cryptography. Springer; 2009. pp. 95-145

[13] Baldi M, Bianchi M, Chiaraluce F, Rosenthal J, Schipani D. Using ldgm codes and sparse syndromes to achieve digital signatures. Post-quantum cryptography. Springer. 2013:1-15

[14] Cover TM. Enumerative source encoding. Information Theory, IEEE Transactions on. 1973;**19**(1):73-77

[15] Sendrier N. Efficient generation of binary words of given weight. Cryptography and Coding. Springer. 1995:184-187

[16] Goloumb G. Run length encoding. Information Theory, IEEE Transactions on. 1966;**12**: 399-401

[17] Sendrier N. Encoding information into constant weight words. In: Information Theory, 2005. ISIT 2005. Proceedings. International Symposium on. IEEE. 2005. pp. 435-438

[18] Heyse S. Low-reiter: Niederreiter encryption scheme for embedded microcontrollers. In: Post-Quantum Cryptography; Springer; 2010. pp. 165-181

[19] Heyse S, Güneysu T. Towards one cycle per bit asymmetric encryption: Code-based cryptography on reconfigurable hardware. In: Cryptographic Hardware and Embedded Systems–CHES 2012; Springer; 2012. pp. 340-355

[20] Courtois NT, Finiasz M, Sendrier N. How to achieve a Mceliece-based digital signature scheme. In: Advances in Cryptology-ASIACRYPT 2001; Springer; 2001. pp. 157-174

[21] Landais G, Sendrier N. CFS software implementation. IACR Cryptology ePrint Archive. 2012;**2012**:132

[22] Finiasz M. Parallel-CFS. In: Selected Areas in Cryptography. Berlin: Springer; 2011. pp. 159-170

[23] Misoczki R, Tillich J-P, Sendrier N, Barreto PS. Mdpc-mceliece: New mceliece variants from moderate density parity check codes. In: 2013 IEEE International Symposium on Information Theory Proceedings (ISIT); IEEE. 2013. pp. 2069-2073

[24] Phesso A, Tillich J-P. An efficient attack on a code-based signature scheme. In: International Workshop on Post-Quantum Cryptography; Springer; 2016. pp. 86-103

[25] Hu J, Cheung RC. An application specific instruction set processor (ASIP) for the Niederreiter cryptosystem. Cryptology ePrint Archive. Report 2015/1172; 2015. http://eprint.iacr.org/2015/1172.pdf

[26] Hu J, Cheung RC, Güneysu T. Compact constant weight coding engines for the code-based cryptography. IEEE Transactions on Circuits and Systems II: Express Briefs. 2017; **64**(9):1092-1096

[27] Kocher PC. Timing attacks on implementations of diffie-hellman, rsa, dss, and other systems. Annual International Cryptology Conference. Springer. 1996:104-113

[28] Dhem J-F, Koeune F, Leroux P-A, Mestré P, Quisquater J-J, Willems J-L. A practical implementation of the timing attack. In: International Conference on Smart Card Research and Advanced Applications; Springer; 1998. pp. 167-182

[29] Heyse S, Von Maurich I, Güneysu T. Smaller keys for code-based cryptography: QC-MDPC Mceliece implementations on embedded devices. In: Cryptographic Hardware and Embedded Systems–CHES 2013; Springer; 2013. pp. 273-292

[30] Beuchat J-L, Sendrier N, Tisserand A, Villard G. FPGA Implementation of a Recently Published Signature Scheme. France Doctoral dissertation, INRIA; 2004

[31] Chen C, Eisenbarth T, Von Maurich I, Steinwandt R. Differential power analysis of a mceliece cryptosystem. In: International Conference on Applied Cryptography and Network Security. Springer; 2015. pp. 538-556

[32] von Maurich I, Güneysu T. Lightweight code-based cryptography: QC-MDPC McEliece encryption on reconfigurable devices. In: Proceedings of the Conference on Design, Automation & Test in Europe. European Design and Automation Association; 2014. p. 38

Chapter 3

Protocol for Multiple Black Hole Attack Avoidance in Mobile Ad Hoc Networks

Rushdi A. Hamamreh

Additional information is available at the end of the chapter

http://dx.doi.org/10.5772/intechopen.73310

Abstract

Mobile ad hoc networks (MANETs) form a new wireless networking paradigm with unique characteristics that give them appreciated interest in a vast range of applications. However, many challenges are facing MANETs including security, routing, transmission range, and dynamically changing topology with high node mobility. Security is considered as the main obstacle for the widespread adoption of MANET applications. Black hole attack is a type of DoS attack that can disrupt the services of the network layer. It has the worst malicious impact on network performance as the number of malicious nodes increases. Several mechanisms and protocols have been proposed to detect and mitigate its effects using different strategies. However, many of these solutions impose more overhead and increase the average end-to-end delay. This chapter proposes an enhanced and modified protocol called "Enhanced RID-AODV," based on a preceding mechanism: RID-AODV. The proposed enhancement is based on creating dynamic blacklists for each node in the network. Each node, according to criteria, depends on the number of mismatches of hash values of received packets as compared with some threshold values, and the sudden change in the round-trip time (RTT) can decide to add or remove other nodes to or from its blacklist. The threshold is a function of mobility (variable threshold) to cancel the effect of normal link failure. Enhanced RID-AODV was implemented in ns-2 simulator and compared with three previous solutions for mitigating multiple black hole attacks in terms of performance metrics. The results show an increase in throughput and packet delivery ratio and a decrease in end-to-end delay and overhead ratio.

Keywords: enhanced RID-AODV, MANET security, multiple black hole attacks, network layer attack

1. Introduction

A mobile ad hoc network (MANET) is a network of mobile nodes that are able to move arbitrarily and are connected by wireless links. It is a self-configuring network that does

not require any preexistent infrastructure such as centralized management or base stations. If two mobile nodes are within each other transmission range, then they can communicate with each other directly; otherwise, the nodes in between have to forward the packet for them. Hence, mobile nodes are not only functioning as hosts but they are also functioning as routers [1, 2].

Because MANETs are infrastructure-less networks with no centralized administration, they can be self-deployed in a short time. The easy deployment of nodes, self-organizing nature, and freedom of mobility make MANETs suitable for a broad range of applications. They can be useful in disaster recovery and emergency operations where there is not enough time or resources to install and configure an infrastructure. They are also used in other applications, for example, in military services, maritime communications, vehicle networks, casual meetings, campus networks, robot networks, etc., [3].

On the other hand, MANETs are vulnerable to various attacks at all layers. So, much research has been conducted on providing security services for MANETs, because security is the main obstacle for the widespread adoption of MANET applications. MANETs are vulnerable in their functionality: intruders can compromise the operation of the network by attacking at any of the physical, MAC, or network layers. The network layer, especially the routing protocol, is vulnerable because of the use of cooperative routing algorithms, the limited computational ability of nodes, the exhaustible node batteries, the lack of clearly defined physical network boundary, and the transient nature of services in the network. Standard information security measures such as encryption and authentication do not provide complete protection; thus intrusion detection and prevention (IDP) mechanisms are widely used to secure MANETs [4].

Attacks in MANET can be divided, according to the criteria that whether they disrupt the operation of a routing protocol or not, into two classes: passive attacks and active attacks. In passive attacks, the attacker attempts to discover valuable information but does not disrupt the operation of the routing protocol. Active attacks, however, involve actions like modification and deletion of exchanging data to absorb packets destined to other nodes to the attacker for analyzing or disabling the network [5].

Black hole attack is a type of active attack that exploits the route reply message (RREP) feature of the routing protocol. A malicious node sends RREP messages without checking its routing table for a fresh route to a destination. A RREP message from a malicious node is the first to arrive at a source node. Hence, a source node updates its routing table for the new route to the particular destination node and discards any other RREP messages from other neighboring nodes or even from the actual destination node. Once a source node saves a route, it starts sending buffered data packets to a malicious node hoping they will be forwarded to a destination node. Nevertheless, a malicious node (performing a black hole attack) drops all data packets rather than forwarding them [6].

So, the black hole attack is a DoS attack that disrupts the services of routing layer by exploiting the route discovery process of AODV. According to many research studies that focus on studying the effects of malicious attacks on network performance, the simulation results show that the black hole attack is more dangerous than other attacks in the network layer [7].

http://dx.doi.org/10.5772/intechopen.73310

Several mechanisms and protocols have been proposed to detect and mitigate its effect using different strategies. However, many of these solutions impose more overhead and increase the average end-to-end delay. In this paper, we propose a modified and enhanced protocol that aims to detect and mitigate the effects of multiple black hole attacks in MANETs. The proposed solution, "Enhanced RID-AODV," was implemented in ns-2 simulator and compared with three previous solutions for mitigating multiple black hole attacks in terms of performance metrics. The results show an increase in throughput and packet delivery ratio and a decrease in end-to-end delay and overhead ratio.

The rest of this paper is organized as follows: Section 2 provides some details about the black hole attack; Section 3 provides the related work in detection and mitigation of black hole attack. The proposed protocol is introduced in Section 4; the simulation and network environment is described in Sections 5 and 6, the analysis and the results are discussed. Finally, the conclusion is presented in Section 7.

2. Black hole attack in MANETs

Routing protocols in mobile ad hoc networks by their nature are distributed routing protocols with the assumption that all nodes in the network will cooperate truly and participate honestly. However, the existence of malicious nodes makes this assumption not true. Such nodes may drop the packets, if they are not the destination, without forwarding them or may disrupt the routing discovery and maintenance processes resulting in abnormal network operation that affects the performance of the network and may cause denial of service [8].

A black hole attack is a kind of denial of service where a malicious node can attract all packets by falsely claiming a fresh route to the destination and then absorb them (drop all packets) without forwarding them to the destination [9].

In reactive routing protocols such as AODV, the destination sequence number (*dest_seq*) is used to describe the freshness of the route. A higher value of *dest_seq* means a fresher route. On receiving a RREQ, an intruder can advertise itself as having the fresher route by sending a route reply (RREP) packet with a new *dest_seq* number larger than the current *dest_seq*

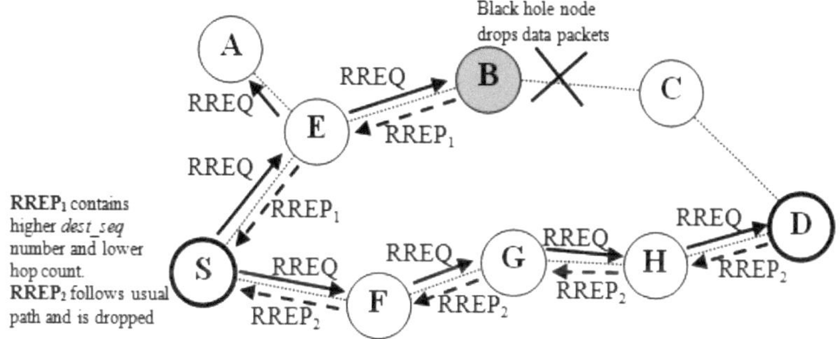

Figure 1. Black hole attack illustration.

number. In this way the intruder becomes part of the route to that destination [10]. **Figure 1** illustrates the black hole attack where nodes S and D are the source and destination, respectively, and node B is the black hole.

A black hole has two properties: First, the node exploits the ad hoc routing protocol to advertise itself as having a valid route to a destination, even though the route is spurious with the intention of intercepting packets. Second, the node consumes the intercepted packets. In an ad hoc network that uses the AODV protocol, a black hole node absorbs the network traffic and drops all packets [9].

3. Materials and methods

Several mechanisms and protocols using different strategies have been proposed to protect MANETs against black hole attacks. In addition, some research studies have focused on studying the effect of malicious nodes on network performance without providing any solutions. Kanthe et al. studied the effect of malicious attacks in mobile ad hoc networks including black hole attack, packet drop attack, and gray hole attack on AODV protocol under different performance metrics: throughput, packet drop rate, and end-to-end delay. It was found that the black hole attack is more dangerous than other attacks mentioned in this paper [7].

Aad et al. provided a quantitative study of the performance impact and scalability of DoS attacks in ad hoc networks. They have also considered the black hole attack, as its impact in ad hoc networks. The authors considered the following as critical performance measures for a system under attack: total system throughput and probability of interception in addition to the system fairness measures and the mean number of hops for a received packet. The simulation results for the impact of black hole node showed that the system has high fairness index with no black hole in the network [11].

Dinesh Mishra et al. analyzed the effects of black hole attack in mobile ad hoc network using AODV and DSR routing protocols. The authors considered the throughput as the main performance measure. Simulation results, by NS-2 simulator, showed that a higher data packet loss when using DSR as compared to AODV. The observation and results showed that DSR data loss is around 55–60% in the presence of black hole attack, while 45–50% in the AODV routing. AODV protocol provides better performance than the DSR in the presence of black holes with minimal additional delay and overhead [12].

Sonja Buchegger and Jean-Yves Le Boudec proposed a robust reputation system for misbehavior detection in mobile ad hoc networks. Nodes have a monitor for observations, reputation records for first-hand and trusted second-hand observations about routing and forwarding behavior of other nodes, trust records to control trust given to received warnings, and a path manager to adapt their behavior according to reputation and to take action against misbehaved nodes. Nodes monitor their neighbors and change the reputation accordingly. When the reputation rating is bad, they take action in routing and forwarding. The routes containing the misbehaved node are either reranked or deleted from the path cache. In addition, once a node has detected a misbehaved node, it informs other nodes by sending an ALARM message [13].

Deng et al. proposed a method to solve the black hole problem. This method is to disable the ability of an intermediate node to reply in a RREP message, so all reply messages should be sent out only by the destination node. This method increases the routing delay, especially for a large network. Besides, a malicious node can take advantage by fabricating a reply message claiming it was sent from the destination node. Another solution was proposed in this paper that depends on using one more route to the intermediate node that replays the RREQ message to check whether the route from the intermediate node to the destination node exists or not. If it does not exist, the reply message from the intermediate node is discarded and an alarm message to the network is sent out. Using this method, the black hole problem was avoided, and further malicious behavior was also prevented. This method cannot prevent multiple black hole attacks [14].

Seungjoon Lee et al. proposed a method to avoid black hole attack based on introducing additional route confirmation messages: route confirmation request (CREQ) and route confirmation reply (CREP). In the proposed method, the intermediate node requests its next hop to send a confirmation message to the source. After receiving both route reply and confirmation message, the source determines the validity of path according to its policy. Simulation results show remarkable improvement in 30% higher delivery ratio. Its drawback is that it cannot detect multiple black hole attacks and the control messages have been increased [15].

Kurosawa et al. proposed an anomaly detection scheme for black hole nodes using dynamic training method in which the training data is updated at regular time intervals. They considered the destination sequence number in order to detect this attack. In normal state, sequence number changes depending on its traffic conditions, and the destination sequence number tends to rise monotonically when the number of connections increases. However, during the attack, the sequence number is increased largely. A statistical method is applied for detection of black hole that is based on the difference between destination sequence numbers of received RREPs. The simulation results of this method showed significant effectiveness in detecting the black hole attack as compared with conventional scheme. Through the simulation, our method shows significant effectiveness in detecting the black hole attack [16].

The solution proposed by Kumar and Selvakumar, focuses on the requirement of a source node to wait unless there is arrival of RREP packet from more than two nodes. When it receives multiple RREPs, the source node checks that there is any share hops or not. The source node will consider the route safe if it finds the share hops. Its drawback is the introduction of time delay it has to wait for the arrival of multiple RREPs before it judges the authentication of node [17].

A lightweight routing protocol IDSAODV was proposed by Dokurer et al. in [18] as a solution for black hole attack problem in MANETs. The authors manually analyzed the output file obtained from simulation and found out very soon after the first RREP from the destination node a second RREP arrived at the source node. Through simulation, they found out that the first RREP was from the black hole node and the second RREP was from the intended destination. At this point, for future simulations, they assumed that the first RREP would always be from black hole node and modified the AODV protocol to ignore the first RREP and send using second RREP route. A RREP caching mechanism to count the second RREP message was added to aodv.cc file in NS-2 [18].

The simulation results demonstrate that IDSAODV improved the PDR in a MANET with a single black hole node, thus proving the successful implementation of the route caching mechanism [18].

Many of the proposed solutions that make the route establishment process longer while the nodes are moving are facing from the link failure problem. Shree and Ogwu in [6] addressed this issue by getting advantage of the reverse AODV (RAODV) routing protocol proposed by Kim et al. in [19]. RAODV discovers route using reverse route discovery procedure where the destination node sends reverse-route request (R-RREQ) messages to its neighbors to find a valid route to the source node after receiving RREQ from source node. Their simulation results of RAODV show that it does improve the performance of AODV in metrics such as packet delivery ratio (PDR), end-to-end delay, and energy consumption [6, 19].

Although RAODV has not been designed to prevent black hole attacks and it was developed with the aim of solving path failure problem, Shree and Ogwu proposed in [6] to use it in mitigating the effects of black hole attacks in ad hoc networks. Therefore, they proposed RID-AODV protocol that combines RAODV (proposed in [19]) and IDSAODV (proposed in [18]) to withstand multiple black hole attacks in client-based WMNs [6].

4. The proposed protocol: enhanced RID-AODV

Routing is an essential operation in all network types, and it has special importance in ad hoc networks, because in such networks, nodes are operating not only as hosts, but they are also operating as routers. Therefore, any breakthrough in the routing process has a direct impact to the performance of the whole network. This is the reason why routing is targeted in many kinds of attacks in MANETs especially black hole attack.

The proposed protocol, "Enhanced RID-AODV," is a modification and enhancement of the RID-AODV protocol proposed in [6]. RID-AODV protocol was proposed as combination of previous two protocols, namely, IDSAODV (which is proposed in [18]) and RAODV (proposed in [19]) as mentioned in the previous section. Therefore, we got all the advantages of the preceding protocols in mitigating the bad impact of the existence of malicious black hole nodes in the ad hoc network. Thus, better results in terms of performance metrics [20].

The detection of the malicious nodes and mitigation their effects can be achieved by creating and maintaining *dynamic blacklist* in each node according to some criteria. Then each non-malicious node will prevent sending or forwarding to the neighboring nodes that exist in its own blacklist either in the forward or reverse path. In other words, each node will not use blacklisted nodes as intermediate nodes. Dynamic blacklist means that each node adds and removes nodes to or from its blacklist automatically according to specific criteria as will be explained in this section.

The criteria for each node to add another node's address in its blacklist is the repetitive mismatch in the hash value of the receiving frames (layer 2 frame) from the same neighboring node. So, each node keeps a counter for each other node that receives a frame from the neighboring nodes. If there is a mismatch between the received hash value and the calculated value, the corresponding counter for the sending (or forwarding) node will be incremented. When the counter reaches some threshold value ($malPcktThreshold$), then the corresponding neighboring node will be blacklisted [21].

Each node keeps small number of counters. If node n_i has p neighboring nodes (p is $\subseteq$ of all nodes) and n_i is receiving from q nodes ($q is \subseteq of p$), then n_i will keep only q counters for this purpose.

In addition, we can get another advantage of the nature of the reverse route discovery procedure in RAODV to create *full path (bidirectional) integrity check implemented in hop-by-hop basis* to detect any modifications on the traversing packets and to detect the causing nodes.

To distinguish between hash value mismatch that may occur as a result of normal link failure, which is from the nature of MANETs due to mobility of nodes that communicate wirelessly or from the existence of malicious nodes, the threshold value $malPcktThreshold$ should be considered as a function of mobility (variable threshold). If the node is moving with relatively high speed, the mismatch of hash values is most likely due to normal link failure, and so the threshold should be high. On the other hand, if there are many hash value mismatches while the node is moving slowly, there is most likely a malicious node. So, the value of $malPcktThreshold$ is directly proportional to the node speed, and it was implemented by using Eq. (1):

$$malPcktThreshold = NodeSpeed + C \tag{1}$$

where C is the threshold value when the node speed is zero.

The malicious node may not act as a black hole all the time; it may become benign for some period of time; then it may (or may not) resume its malicious activities. So, when a node adds another node's address to its blacklist, the blacklisted node will not stay in its blacklist forever. However, it will be blacklisted for a previously specified period of time. So, when a node is added to another node's blacklist, not only the address of the blacklist is added but also the expiry time for that node to be released from that blacklist. The blacklisted node expiry time is computed using Eq. (2):

$$blkListedNodeExpTime = CURRENT_{TIME} + blockingPeriod \tag{2}$$

Each time the node wants to send (or forward) a packet to a neighboring node, it will check if it is blacklisted, and if so it will also check the expiry time for that node. If it's expired, it will be removed from the blacklist of that node, and its corresponding counter and expiry timer will be reset. Because of that it is a dynamic blacklist.

When a node wants to send (or forward) a packet, in either the forward path or reverse path, it will check the routing table to decide what is the next hop. Then it will check if the next hop is blacklisted or not; if it's blacklisted, it will check the blacklist expiry time. If the next hop node is still blacklisted, then the node will remove that node from its neighbor list and run the handle link failure procedure. Then the node will try to send (or forward) the packet by using another path.

As a result, we can get a secure path that avoids the black hole malicious nodes during routing packet as shown in **Figure 2**.

The criterion for the reverse path is the round-trip time (RTT). RTT is the length of time it takes the RREQ to be sent (or forwarded) plus the length of time it takes for the R-RREQ to be received by the node. As we assumed that all the nodes are trusted, we can measure RTT in the normal behavior and use it as a reference. Any change in this value indicates that the reply was not from the original destination, so this value can be used to detect the malicious node.

The node will first measure round-trip time (RTT). Then it will calculate the average hop-to-hop time (T_{h-h}) using Eq. (3):

$$T_{h-h} = \frac{RTT}{2 * hopcount} \tag{3}$$

Now, the New RTT (RTT_{next}) should satisfy the following condition:

$$RTT - \frac{T_{h-h}}{2} < RTT_{next} < RTT + \frac{T_{h-h}}{2} \tag{4}$$

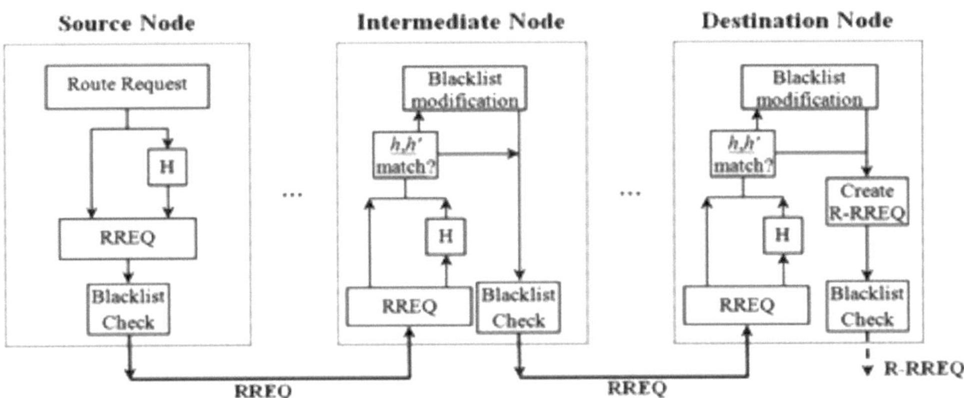

Figure 2. Secure routing path.

The sequence diagram of the Enhanced RID-AODV protocol is shown in **Figure 3**. *RTT* values are shown in normal behavior and in malicious behavior.

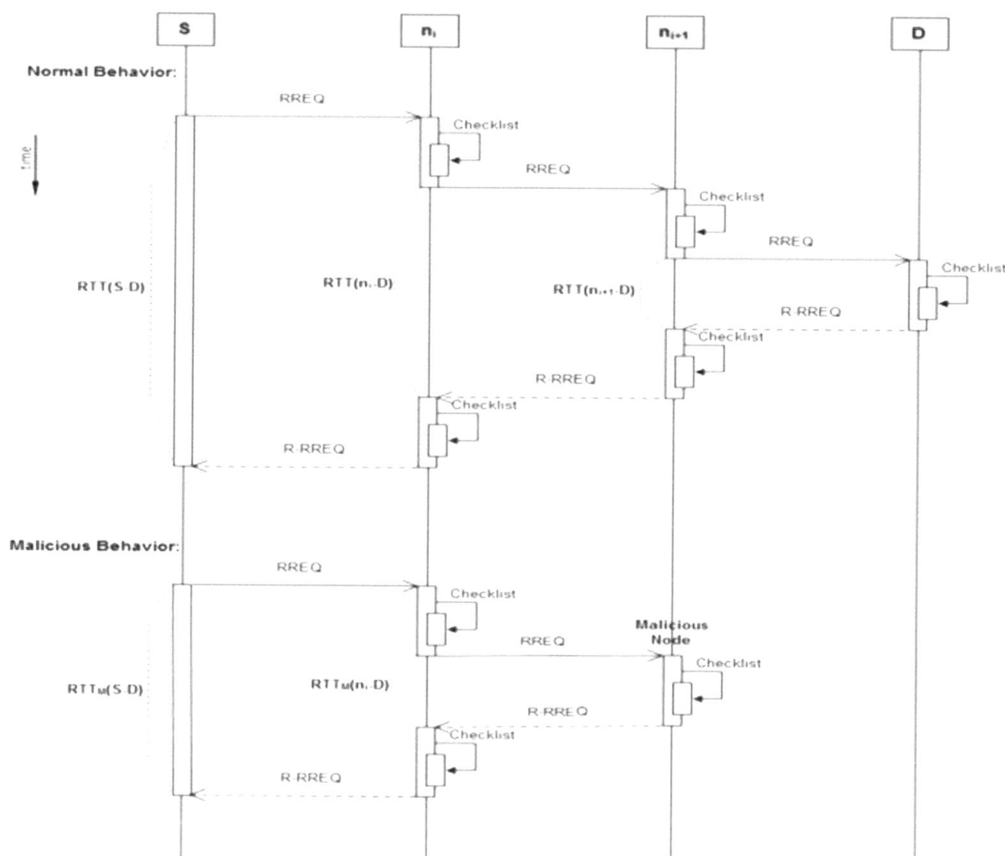

Figure 3. Sequence diagram for the Enhanced RID-AODV.

Pseudocode for the proposed protocol: How the node decides to add or remove other nodes in its blacklist:

1. Generate new hash value ($NewHash$).
2. Compare the generated hash value New_{Hash} with the received hash value with the packet $HashVal$.
3. if($NewHash \neq HashVal$ then, $incrmalNodeCouter(PrevHopAddr)$
4. Check the speed of the node ($NodeSpeed$).
5. Compute the threshold that will be used to consider a node as blacklisted $malPcktThreshold = NodeSpeed + C$
6. *//To add a node to a blacklist*
   if $(isBlacklisted(NextHop) = FALSE \wedge malNodeCouter(NextHop) > malPcktThreshold)$
   then,
   a. $addBlackList(NextHop)$.
   b. $blkListedNodeExpTime(NextHop) = CURRENT_{TIME} + BlockingPeriod$

Figure 4. Pseudocode for the proposed protocol: how the node decides to add other nodes in its blacklist.

Pseudocode for the proposed protocol: How the node decides to add or remove other nodes in its blacklist:

//To remove a node from a blacklist

if $\left(isBlaklisted\left(NextHop\right)=TRUE \wedge CURRENT_{TIME} > BlkListedNodeExpTime\left(NextHop\right)\right)$

then,

a. $removeBlackList\left(NextHop\right)$.
b. $malNodeCouter\left(NextHop\right)=0$
c. $blkListedNodeExpTime\left(NextHop\right)=0$

Figure 5. Pseudocode for the proposed protocol: how the node decides to remove a node from its blacklist.

Pseudocode for the proposed protocol: How the node behaves when sending or forwarding a packet:

if($isBlacklisted\left(NextHop\right)=TRUE$

then,

// Generate route error message

$sendRERR$

Figure 6. Pseudocode for the proposed protocol: how the node behaves when sending or forwarding a packet.

Figure 7. Flowchart of the Enhanced RID-AODV protocol.

In our protocol we used one-way hashing function on the level of packets in the routing discovery control messages. The purpose of using a hash function is to produce a "fingerprint" of the message. This fingerprint will be used for route request (RREQ) *packet authentication* and *integrity check* in each hop while traversing from source node to the destination node and for reverse route request (R-RREQ) from destination to source, resulting in a two-way (bidirectional) control packet authentication and integrity check. To implement the Enhanced RID-AODV protocol, a new field was added in the route request (RREQ) and reverse route request (R-RREQ).

The pseudocodes for the Enhanced RID-AODV protocol are presented in **Figures 4–6**.

The flowchart for the Enhanced RID-AODV protocol is illustrated in **Figure 7**.

5. Simulation and network environment

Network Simulator version 2 (NS-2) was adopted in this research study because it is one of the most popular network simulators that are appropriate to simulate the wireless networks. Ns-2 is an open-source discrete event-driven simulator that is written in C++ language. During the simulation the packet header (*aodv_packet.h* file) of the AODV route request and route reply (changed to route reverse request) is modified to hold the hash value ($Hash_{Val}$) with packet. In addition to that, the files *aodv.h* and *aodv.cc* were modified to implement the Enhanced RID-AODV protocol together with previous protocols. Also, files*/common/node.h* and */common/node.cc* have been modified to hold the q counters and the blacklists inside each node. Simulation was carried out by referring to many resources including but not limited to references [22–24].

The simulation area is a square field of 1000 × 1000 m with fixed sender and receiver nodes that communicate using intermediate mobile nodes, which are moving randomly during simulation time (these random movements were generated using *setdest* tool), and the intermediate nodes are sending random traffic pattern among each other (created using *cbrgen.tcl* command). The sender and receiver were placed in points (200,200) and (800,800), respectively. So they are out of the transmission range of each other, and all traffic between them is through the moving intermediate nodes. The parameter considered in this simulation is given in **Table 1**.

In this research, the Enhanced RID-AODV protocol together with four preceding protocols was implemented and simulated with the same environment parameters to be able to make a comparison among them. That includes the genuine AODV protocol with simulation of black hole malicious nodes, the IDSAODV protocol, RAODV protocol, RID-AODV protocol, and our proposed protocol which is Enhanced RID-AODV. For each protocol many scenarios were generated to simulate the existence of different numbers of malicious nodes in order to study the effect of multiple malicious nodes on network performance and the effectiveness of each protocol to compare among these protocols; we made as many combinations of nodes to act as malicious nodes, and then we computed the average of the results.

Parameter	Value
Simulator	ns-2
Routing protocol	AODV, IDSAODV, R-AODV, RID-AODV, Enhanced RID-AODV
Simulation time	100 sec
Simulation area	1000 × 1000 m
Number of nodes	40
Number of malicious nodes	0, 1, 2, 3, 4, 5, 6, 7
Sender node	Fixed at point (200,200)
Receiver node	Fixed at point (800,800)
Intermediate nodes	Moving randomly
Maximum speed of mobile nodes	40 m/s
Data rate	50 Kb/s
Pause time	0 sec
Transport type	UDP, CBR
Data packet size	Default
MAC protocol	IEEE 802.11

Table 1. Parameters used in simulation.

5.1. Performance metrics

Four performance metrics were considered and computed as the average of many cases in all scenarios of multiple malicious nodes for all the protocols in this research. Four separate scripts were generated to compute these performance metrics using *awk* command:

- **Throughput**: the amount of data transferred over the period of time expressed in kilobits per second (kbps). Throughput has been calculated using Eq. (5):

$$Throughput = \frac{\sum ReceivedDataPackets}{SimulationTime} \tag{5}$$

- **Packet delivery ratio (PDR)**: the percentage ratio of the total number of data packets received by the destination node to the number of data packets sent by the source node as in Eq. (6):

$$PDR = \frac{\sum NumberofReceivedDataPackets}{\sum NumberofSentDataPackets} * 100 \tag{6}$$

- **Average end-to-end delay**: the average delay between the sending of the data packet by the source node and its receipt at the destination node. This includes all the delays caused during route acquisition, buffering and processing at intermediate nodes, retransmission delays at the MAC layer, etc. The average end-to-end delay was computed using Eq. (7):

http://dx.doi.org/10.5772/intechopen.73310

$$Avg_{E2E_{Delay}} = \frac{\sum_{i=1}^{n}(ReceiveTimeofP_i - SentTimeofP_i)}{NumberofReceivedPacket} \tag{7}$$

where i is the packet index and n the last packet in the message.

- **Overhead ratio**: the ratio of the total number of control packets sent at the routing level and the total number of packets sent from the source node as in Eq. (8):

$$OverheadRatio = 1 - \frac{NumberofDataPacketsSentatRTR}{NumberofAllPacketsSentatRTR} \tag{8}$$

6. Results and analysis

Figure 8 shows the results of the throughput for the case of the existence of black hole nodes (as the number of black hole nodes increases up to seven malicious nodes) for the genuine AODV and the four solutions: IDSAODV, R-AODV, RIS-AODV, and Enhanced RID-AODV.

Figure 8 shows the effects of increasing the number of malicious nodes in the network on the throughput are clear. One black hole in the network has a huge impact in decreasing the throughput, and few numbers of malicious nodes are able to prevent all traffic from reaching the destination. Previous protocols provide sole improvements on the throughput; however, the Enhanced RID-AODV protocol provides more improvement to throughput that takes advantages from its enhancements and from the preceding protocols in stability and robustness in avoiding multiple black hole nodes.

The packet delivery ratio (PDR) was computed; the results are shown in **Figure 9**.

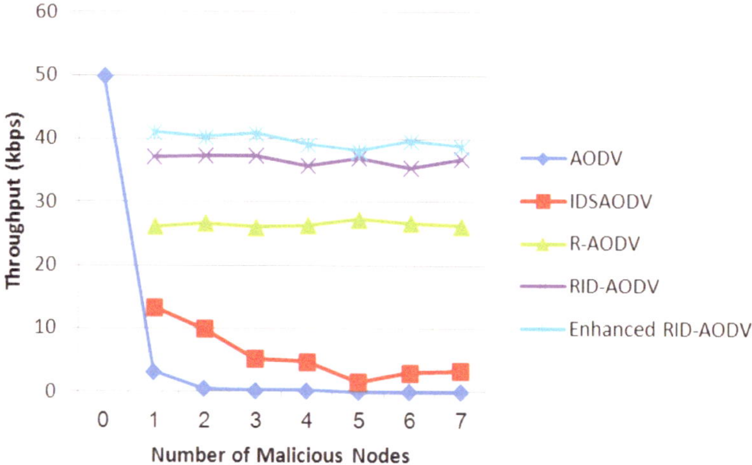

Figure 8. Throughput vs. number of malicious nodes for different protocols.

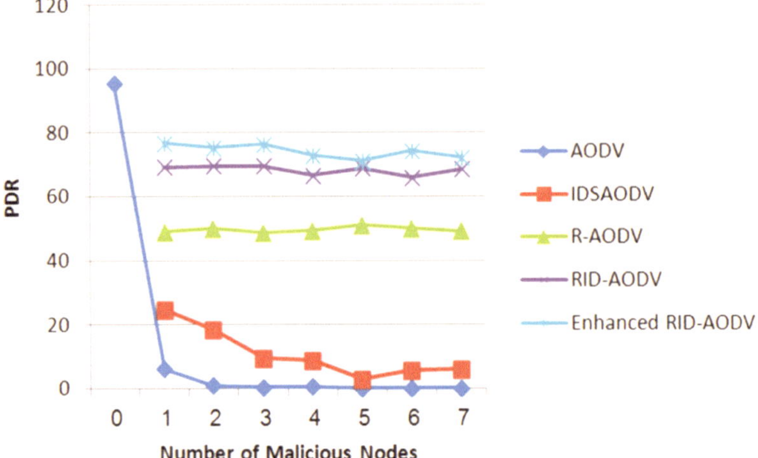

Figure 9. PDR vs. number of malicious nodes for different protocols.

The impact of malicious nodes in dropping the packets to reduce the received packets is obvious. Only one black hole node in the network is able to reduce the PDR to around 10% of the original PDR. We can notice the improvements provided by the different protocols in the research.

One of the major improvements of the Enhanced RID-AODV is decreasing the average end-to-end delay. The results are illustrated in **Figure 10**.

The previous protocols had an impact in increasing the average end-to-end delay with the increase in the throughput and PDR. However, in the Enhanced RID-AODV, due to the use of blacklists, the nodes choose the optimized path. As a result the average end-to-end delay has decreased as compared to RID-AODV. This is an important improvement because time is a significant factor in ad hoc networks.

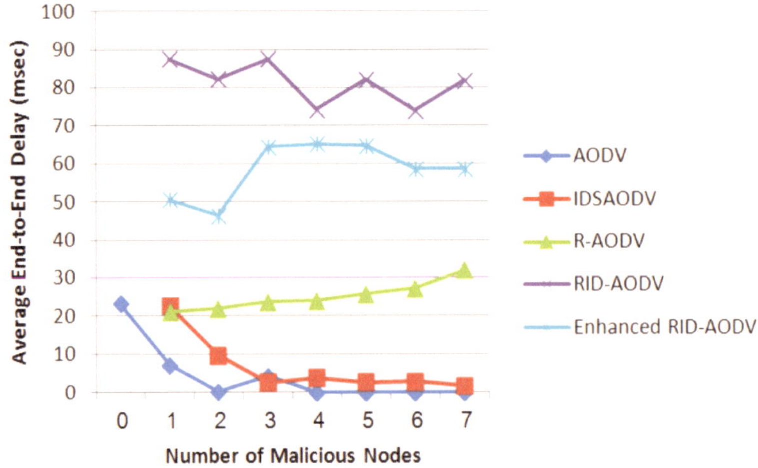

Figure 10. Average end-to-end delay vs. number of malicious nodes for different protocols.

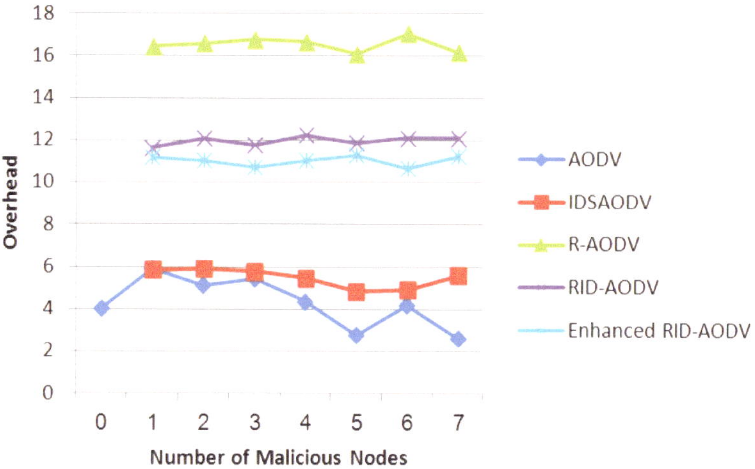

Figure 11. Overhead ratio vs. number of malicious nodes for different protocols.

Also the overhead ratio has been improved by the proposed protocol as shown in **Figure 11**.

The previous protocols impose more overhead. The increase of the overhead ratio is mainly due to R-RREQ control message. However, in Enhanced RID-AODV, and as a result of applying blacklists in the intermediate nodes, the overhead ratio has decreased.

7. Conclusion

Several mechanisms and protocols have been proposed to detect and mitigate the effects of multiple black hole attack using different strategies. However, many of these solutions impose more overhead and increase the average end-to-end delay. In this paper a new mechanism, called "Enhanced RID-AODV," was proposed to detect and mitigate the effects of multiple black hole attacks in MANETs aiming to increase the throughput and PDR while decreasing the average end-to-end delay and overhead. It is an enhanced and modified version of a previously proposed mechanism called RID-AODV. RID-AODV is a combination of two other protocols: RAODV and IDSAODV.

According to the simulation results, Enhanced RID-AODV provides higher throughput and higher packet delivery ratio than its preceding version. Also, the dynamic blacklists provide positive effects in decreasing the overhead ratio and the end-to-end delay.

Author details

Rushdi A. Hamamreh

Address all correspondence to: rhamamreh@eng.alquds.edu

Computer Engineering Department, Al-Quds University, Israel

References

[1] Corson S, Macker J. Mobile Ad hoc Networking (MANET): Routing Protocol Performance Issues and Evaluation Considerations. RFC: 2501, IETF. [Online]. Available: http://tools.ietf.org/html/rfc2501

[2] Bakshi A, Sharma AK, Mishra A. Significance of mobile AD-HOC networks (MANETS). International Journal of Innovative Technology and Exploring Engineering (IJITEE). March 2013;**2**(4). ISSN: 2278-3075

[3] Kannhavong B, Nakayama H, Nemoto Y, Kato N, Jamalipour A. A survey of routing attacks in mobile ad hoc networks. IEEE Wireless Communications. October 2007; **14**(5):85-91

[4] Nadeem A, Howarth MP. A survey of MANET Intrusion Detection & Prevention Approaches for network layer attacks. IEEE Communications Surveys & Tutorials. 2013

[5] Behzad S, Jamali S. A survey over black hole attack detection in mobile ad hoc network. International Journal of Computer Science and Network Security (IJCSNS). March 2015;**15**(3)

[6] Shree O, Ogwu FJ. A proposal for mitigating multiple black-hole attack in wireless mesh networks. Wireless Sensor Network. 2013;**5**(4):76-83

[7] Kanthe A, Simunic D, Prasad R. Effects of Malicious Attacks in Mobile Ad-hoc Networks. IEEE International Conference on Computational Intelligence and Computing Research, ISBN:978-1-4673-2481-6,18-20, December 2012, Coimbatore, India; 2012

[8] Ehsan H, Khan FA. Malicious AODV. Implementation and Analysis of Routing Attacks in MANETs. 11th International Conference on Trust, Security and Privacy in Computing and Communications. IEEE. 2012

[9] Tamilselvan L, Sankaranarayanan V. Prevention of co-operative black hole attack in MANET. Journal of Networks. MAY 2008;**3**(5):15-20

[10] kurosawa S, Jamalipour A. Detecting blackhole attack on AODV-based mobile ad hoc networks by dynamic learning method. International Journal of Network Security. Nov 2007;**5**:338-346

[11] Aad I, Hubaux PJ, Knightly WE. Impact of denial-of-service attacks on ad-hoc networks. IEEE-ACM Transactions on Networking. 2008;**16**(4):791-802

[12] Mishra D, Jain KY, Agarwal S. "Behavior analysis of malicious node in the different routing algorithms in mobile ad hoc network (MANET)", Proceeding from ACT'09: IEEE advances in computing. Control and Telecommunication Technologies, Trivandrum. December 2009;**28-29**:621-623

[13] Buchegger S, Boudec JYL. A Robust Reputation System for Mobile Ad-hoc Networks. Technical Report, IC/2003/50, EPFL/IC/LCA. Lausanne, Switzerland. July 2003

[14] Deng H, Li W, Agrawal DP. Routing security in wireless Ad Hoc networks. Cincinnati University of Cincinnati, OH, USA; IEEE Communications Magazine. ISSN: 0163-6804, Vol.40, Oct. 2002. pp.70-75

[15] Lee S, Han B, Shin M. Robust Routing in Wireless Ad Hoc Networks. 2002 International Conference on Parallel Processing Workshops. Vancouver, Canada; Aug 2002. pp. 73-78 DOI: 10.1109/ICPPW.2002.1039714

[16] Kurosawa S, Nakayama H, Kat N, Jamalipour A, Nemoto Y. Detecting blackhole attack on AODV-based mobile ad hoc networks by dynamic learning method. International Journal of Network Security. Nov. 2007;**5**(3):338-346

[17] P.A.R Kumar, S.Selvakumar, "Distributed denial-of-service (DDoS) threat in collaborative environment - a survey on DDoS attack tools and Traceback mechanisms", IEEE International Advance Computing Conference (IACC 2009), pp. 1275-1280, March, 2009

[18] Dokurer S, Erten YM, Can EA. Performance analysis of ad-hoc networks under black hole attacks. Proceeding from SECON'07: IEEE Southeast Conference. Richmond, 22-25 March 2007, pp. 148-153

[19] Kim C, Talipov E, Ahn BA reverse AODV routing protocol in ad hoc mobile networks. The International Conference on Emerging Directions in Embedded and Ubiquitous Computing (EUC'06). Seoul, 1-4 August 2006, pp. 522-531. Springer, 2006

[20] Salem A, Hamamreh R. Efficient mechanism for mitigating multiple black hole attacks in MANETs. Journal of Theoretical and Applied Information Technology (JATIT). Jan 2016;**83**(1):156-164

[21] Hamamreh R, Jamoos M, Zagha R. DILH: Data integrity using linear combination for hash algorithm. ICITeS-Edas-1569740315-18

[22] The Network Simulator ns-2. [Online]. Available: http://www.isi.edu/nsnam/ns

[23] Hegde N, Manvi S. Simulation of wireless sensor network security model using NS2. International Journal of Latest Trends in Engineering and Technology (IJLTET). May 2014;**4**

[24] Manikandan C, Parameshwaran R, Hariharan K, Kalaimani N, Sridhar KP. Combined security and integrity agent integration into NS-2 for wired, wireless and sensor networks. Australian Journal of Basic and Applied Sciences. 2013;**7**(7):376-382. ISSN 1991-8178

Chapter 4

A Survey of Machine Learning Techniques for Behavioral-Based Biometric User Authentication

Nurul Afnan Mahadi,
Mohamad Afendee Mohamed,
Amirul Ihsan Mohamad, Mokhairi Makhtar,
Mohd Fadzil Abdul Kadir and Mustafa Mamat

Additional information is available at the end of the chapter

http://dx.doi.org/10.5772/intechopen.76685

Abstract

Authentication is a way to enable an individual to be uniquely identified usually based on passwords and personal identification number (PIN). The main problems of such authentication techniques are the unwillingness of the users to remember long and challenging combinations of numbers, letters, and symbols that can be lost, forged, stolen, or forgotten. In this paper, we investigate the current advances in the use of behavioral-based biometrics for user authentication. The application of behavioral-based biometric authentication basically contains three major modules, namely, data capture, feature extraction, and classifier. This application is focusing on extracting the behavioral features related to the user and using these features for authentication measure. The objective is to determine the classifier techniques that mostly are used for data analysis during authentication process. From the comparison, we anticipate to discover the gap for improving the performance of behavioral-based biometric authentication. Additionally, we highlight the set of classifier techniques that are best performing for behavioral-based biometric authentication.

Keywords: continuous authentication, behavioral biometric, machine learning, classification, clustering

1. Introduction

Over the past decade, the field of computer security has evolved along with the changing nature of technology. Computer security comprises of measures and controls that ensure the goals of information security that are confidentiality, integrity, and availability, defined over hardware, software, firmware, and information being processed, stored, and communicated,

are achieved [1]. These goals of information security, also known as CIA triad, is a benchmark model used to evaluate the physical, logical, and perceptual security of information in an organization [2, 3]. The elements of the triad are considered as the three most crucial components of information security. It can have serious effects for an organization if any one of this triad is breachable.

Confidentiality is roughly equivalent to privacy or secrecy which offers prevention of the sensitive information from disclosure by unauthorized individuals or systems [4]. By and large, it is also the one which is attacked most often. Cryptography via encryption algorithms is commonly used to ensure the confidentiality of data in storage or transferred from one computer to another.

Integrity is typically described as the trustworthiness, accuracy, and consistency of data in which the data itself cannot be altered or modified undetectable by unauthorized user [4]. Cryptography plays a major role in ensuring data integrity. This is done by hashing the original data and transmitting the data and the hash to the recipient followed by another hashing on the received data and comparison with the received hash to verify its integrity.

Availability is defined as the security controls required to ensure that the information concerned is readily accessible to the authorized parties when they request it [1]. Denial of service (DoS) attack can be a good example of many threats to this security controls. DoS renders the system to an unavailable state to serving legitimate request by making the server fully utilized the processing power, bandwidth, and memory to handle request mostly mounted by this attack.

Last but not least, authentication is a key point to provide effective information security. Authentication process verifies the identity of a user, process, or device and allows only legal users to use the resources and services in an authorized manner while denying all illegal ones [1].

Nowadays, user authentication is an issue and thus a challenge that becomes more important than ever before [5]. For an online banking system, it is very important to secure the users' accounts and protect their assets and personal information from malicious hands due to highly sensitiveness of data held inside. There are many existing authentication methods; in general, they are categorized into knowledge-based method, possession-based method, and biometric-based method. For sure, all of the methods have their own uniqueness (strengths and weaknesses); however, the environment determines which authentication approach is best suited.

When talking about the authentication in general, two types of well-known approaches have been proposed in the literature, namely, continuous authentication approach and static authentication approach [6]. Continuous authentication approach which can also be acknowledged as dynamic authentication verifies users repeatedly throughout the entire session [7]. The benefit of this approach is that the system is able to continuously monitor if there is any unauthorized access that occurs.

Meanwhile, static authentication approach collect data from the user and verify their access and privileges in manipulating the data, for example, at the login time [7]. This accessing service will be valid until the user logs out from the session. The combination of username and password is a popular method for static authentication. Nevertheless, there is a drawback for static authentication in which this approach will authenticate the user only at the beginning of each session. The system will remain unnoticeable if there is any change of user in case of attacks [6].

In this paper, we survey the most recent advancement in biometric authentication system. However, our focuses are only on behavioral-based biometric authentication. In order to evaluate the accuracy of behavioral-based biometric authentication [8], there are three common measurements which are false rejection rate (FRR), the percentage of users' wrongly denied access to a system; false acceptance rate (FAR), the percentage of users wrongly authorized by a system; and equal error rate (EER), the value of the FRR and FAR when a system is tuned to have an equal FAR and FRR. Generally, in order for the authentication system to be more practical, it must have the following features that are accuracy, quick response, and difficult to be forged [9].

The remainder of this article is organized as follows: Section 2 discusses the biometric authentication. The subtopic in this section described the taxonomy of user authentication methods in each category emphasizing on their advantages and disadvantages. The description of behavioral-based biometric authentication system for every paper is discussed in details. Section 3 presented a discussion and future research direction in the development of behavioral-based biometric authentication system. Finally, Section 4 concludes the paper.

2. Authentication

2.1. User authentication methods

The most important key for the authentication process is the uniqueness of security measures, which in general can be categorized into something a user knows (password), something a user has (smart card), or something a user is (biometrics) [10–13]. Some examples of knowledge-based method, possession-based method, and biometric-based method can be found in **Figure 1**.

2.1.1. Knowledge-based method

Knowledge-based technique is commonly used to secure the access for systems [14]. The two famous examples are the pin and password. The password is normally entered at the beginning of any communication or operation which is only allowed if user has the correct one. The benefits for using conventional password are no specialized personnel required, simple, easy to use, and easy to remember. Unfortunately, passwords have many problems in that it is highly vulnerable to brute force attacks, password guessing, and key-loggers. The drawback is that once the password is compromised, an opponent can easily exploit a victim's account [15].

The marbles gap approach which comprises of password in a form of arbitrary sequence of marbles during authentication process can be found in [16]. The user needs to drag the digits in the right direction into the center of the screen. After that, it immediately reappears on the prior position. In order to leave smudge traces, three graphic-based authentication methods were implemented, which are one grid-based and two randomized graphical approaches.

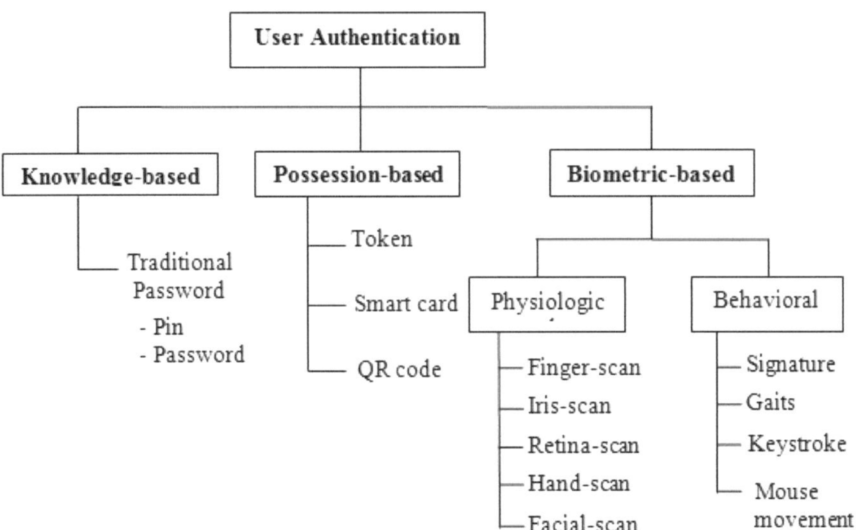

Figure 1. Taxonomy of user authentication methods.

Another authentication scheme for smartphone was established by using the matrix values of image [17]. This approach requires synchronization in advance between the smartphone and the service server. For the task of authentication, the user must react to the service server by inputting an existing combination of text-based and graphic-based passwords and thus providing better accuracy.

Ref. [18] proposed a location-based authentication approach using smartphone. The static (captured at login session) and continuous (captured during the session) location information were used. The two different locations of APIs were utilized during location verification. The location was verified and compared prior deciding whether the user is valid or not. This system can provoke errors during verification process caused by overlapping in location. Therefore, the security of the system introduced depends on the effectiveness of location verification.

Ref. [19] presented the physical proximity to guarantee security using a modulated illumination of smartphone screens to transmit PIN. The user enters a PIN on smartphone. By using a cheap bespoke receiver unit, the PIN is transmitted via temporary patterns of light on the screen. This approach was the right choice to ensure confidentiality against man-in-the-middle attacks.

The hybrid graphical password approach which is the mixture of recall and recognition-based schemes provided more secure system according to the use of graphical and textual password [20]. During registration phase, the user selects a username and a textual password and then chooses an object as password by drawing. All the information is stored in a database. During the authentication process, the user enters username and textual password and then draws the pre-selected objects. As expected, this scheme is not intended for users without drawing capability.

Table 1 shows a summary of various existing user authentication schemes that falls under knowledge-based category listed with advantages and disadvantages. Due to these advantages, the area of knowledge-based method for user authentication becomes less unpopular for exploration by the researchers.

Author	Knowledge	Approach	Advantages	Disadvantages
[16]	Graphical password	The marbles authentication method	This method has no upper restriction for the password space	The pattern of key arrangement must be recognized by the user
[17]	Graphical password	Matrix values of image	Provides more accuracy caused by the combination of sensors	Power consumption
[18]	Location	Location-based authentication	• Used the mobile function • Easy to use	Can provoke errors in verification caused by the overlapping in location
[19]	PIN	A modulated illumination of mobile device screens to transmit PIN	Assures confidentiality against attacks	Light sensor works within limited geographic scope
[20]	Graphical password	Recall and recognition-based schemes	More secure caused by the combination of graphical and textual password	Can provoke login error if the user does not have drawing capability

Table 1. Summary of knowledge-based method.

2.1.2. Possession-based method

The usages of traditional password have already been indicated as not sufficiently secure and inconvenient as a security measure. The possession-based method was proven to eradicate the risk of an attacker to guess passwords and is predicted to raise the level of security to data. This method makes use of things the user personally possesses such as token, smart card, and QR code.

Any objects or devices that can be used during authentication process are called hardware tokens. They are available in various forms such as a mobile device [21] or an easy-access device (key fobs and smartphones). The smart card reader (NFC-enabled smartphones) approach has been introduced with the combination of PIN and smart card [22]. The PIN is managed as a temporary PIN. The use of temporary PIN reduces the chance for an attacker to distinguish the permanent PIN.

The user authentication using QR code identification approach was implemented in this system [23]. During verification phase, the user makes a request from the server; in return, the server will extract the information about that user. The benefit of this approach is that it is known to be faster than the certificate system.

A summary of possession-based category is shown in **Table 2**. Possession-based methods are proven to eradicate the risk of an attacker to guess passwords easily from knowledge-based method. Since the token is needed to be present during the authentication process, the drawbacks of physical token are that, from the stolen or lost token, an attacker might gain an authorized access. Thus, the possession-based method for user authentication can still be considered as weak.

2.1.3. Biometric-based method

The use of human characteristics is the best solution compared to the user that personally knows and possesses [14]. In other words, biometric-based method cannot be forgotten or lost

Author	Possesses	Approach	Advantages	Disadvantages
[22]	PIN + smart card	Smart card reader (NFC-enabled smartphones)	The use of a temporary pin will reduce the chance for an attacker to detect the permanent pin	Public terminal or computer is required as an input and output device for smart cards
[21]	• Acoustic token • Magnetic token	Sound waves and static magnetic fields	Less prone to snooping	A sharp drop in the strength of the magnetic field formed can cause complications to the user
[23]	QR code	QR code identifying for user authentication	• Easy to use • Low cost • Reduces the memorization of human	—

Table 2. Summary of possession-based method.

in contrast to token, smart card, and password [24]. A biometric system is basically a pattern recognition system that recognizes a person based on a feature vector derived from a specific physiological or behavioral characteristic that the person possesses or exhibits [25]. These authentication methods identify the user as themselves based on measurable physiological or behavioral characteristics.

2.1.3.1. Physical biometrics

Various technologies of physiological biometrics including finger scan, iris scan, retina scan, hand scan, and facial scan have been proposed and developed using measurements from the human body. There was evidence that the best accuracy can be obtained by using the physical biometric-based method. **Table 3** shows a summary of biometric-based method (physical biometric) for user authentication.

Fingerprint is the most famous features in biometric-based method and has shown to exhibit the best performance among others. Some of the approaches under fingerprint are of edge-based approach [26] and the rule mining approach [27], as well as the technique of image preprocessing region segmentation [28]. The advantages of using fingerprint are the ease of use and high in authentication accuracy. Nowadays, the fingerprint scanner is used widely among the user.

The concept of facial recognition technique through a vertical pose recovery fast semi-3D face [29] and fragile watermarking based on chaos theory [30] provided an impressive accuracy rate. Moreover, an extra security measure is achievable with the combination of this technique and other user authentication methods such as PIN.

Ref. [31] introduced a Daubechies wavelet transform approach to increase the performance rate for iris recognition. The iris is found to be the most accurate feature and being neither duplicable. Even so, when there are obstacles during the scanning process, the decision on recognition may be disrupted.

2.1.3.2. *Behavioral biometric*

The other group of biometric-based method is the behavioral biometrics, where users are identified based on their human actions such as signature, gaits (the way humans walk), keystroke dynamics (typing styles), and mouse dynamics [32].

Author	Recognition	Approach	Advantages	Disadvantages
[26]	Finger scan	Edge-based approach	Ease of use	Sensitive to camera limitations
[27]	Finger scan	Rule mining	Good in case of phone loss	Bad performance
[28]	Finger scan	Image preprocessing region segmentation	Ease of use	The higher templates that save in enrollment database, the execution time for the verification increases
[29]	Facial scan	Vertical pose recovery Fast semi-3D face	Extra security caused by combining with PIN	High energy consumption
[30]	Facial scan	Fragile watermarking based on chaos theory	Fast speed of authentication process	Not completely secured compared to other techniques
[31]	Iris scan	Daubechies wavelet transform	Increase the recognition of performance rate	Time- and energy-consuming

Table 3. Summary of biometric-based method (physical biometric).

Author	Recognition	Approach	Advantages	Disadvantages
[33]	Gaits	Linear regression classifier (KNN)	Biometric-based authentication with the same efficiency	Depends on the ideal conditions that the owner holds and operates the device in the same style all the time
[34]	Gaits	Classifier (KNN)	Do not involve explicit user interaction during verification process	Requires the punctual calibration of accelerator
[36]	Keystroke dynamics	SVM	Quick and easy configuration of individual thresholds without impostors' data	Large number of data required
[37]	Keystroke dynamics	SVM	The cheapest and easiest for the implementation process	Wasting of time for the user during enrollment process
[38]	Keystroke dynamics	Random forest	• Low cost • Replaceable in the event of compromise	Not sufficient for a high-security environment
[40]	Signature	Fuzzy	Well established for automatic signature verification	—
[39]	Signature	SVM	—	• Limited number of samples to be used for learning • The ability of the system to discriminate the forgeries

Table 4. Summary of biometric-based method (behavioral biometric).

In general, the direction of movement is detected by the magnetometer, while the gait recognition is detected by the gyroscopic sensor and accelerometer [33, 34]. For verification purposes, these authors used the same classifier, which is the K-nearest neighbor (K-NN). The gait recognition has a similar efficiency to the other biometric-based authentication. Nevertheless, the user is required to walk for a certain distance before the process of verification can occur.

Keystroke dynamics is one of the automated methods for verifying the identity of the user based on the manner and rhythm of typing on the keyboard [35]. In paper [36, 37], the authors used the support vector machine (SVM) as a classifier for the development of the system. Another approach that is usually used for the implementation of keystroke dynamics is random forest which can be found in [38].

Signature recognition is another user authentication scheme that works by analyzing handwriting style, in particular the signature. In the offline signature verification, [39] introduced the support vector machine (SVM) classifier, while [40] proposed fuzzy modeling based on the Takagi-Sugeno (TS) model. **Table 4** shows a summary of biometric-based method (behavioral biometric) for user authentication.

3. Behavioral-based biometric authentication

This section aims to find the good techniques for behavioral-based biometric authentication. **Figure 2** shows the various machine learning techniques that can generally be categorized into supervised (classification) and unsupervised (clustering).

Supervised machine learning can be used to classify the data much more accurately. In literatures, researchers have used classification techniques such as K-nearest neighbor (K-NN) [41], multilayer perceptron (MLP) [42], dynamic time warping (DTW) [43], neural network [7, 5, 44], decision tree algorithm [45], normalization and leave-one-out method [46], and support vector machine (SVM) [9, 47, 48]. These techniques have improved the performance of the system, and the results have shown some significant achievements in their respective domains. Meanwhile, unsupervised machine learning can be used to perform data reduction task by filtering out unrepresentative data. The data which will not be able to cluster correctly can be considered as outlier's data. After the reduction task, the classification result is expected to achieve optimal solution. The clustering algorithm can be further subcategorized into flat/partitioning-based and hierarchical-based clustering algorithm [49, 50].

The essential objective for the implementation of the behavioral-based biometric authentication is to acquire the accuracy and also to improve the performance of the system. This goal leads to the creation of a great classifier technique to solve the accuracy problems related to biometric authentication.

Ref. [47] developed an android application using touch-swipe biometric approach. In this work, touchscreen and motion data were collected through a physiological questionnaire. Parameters that are measured were duration, average velocity, mean X, mean Y, mean Z,

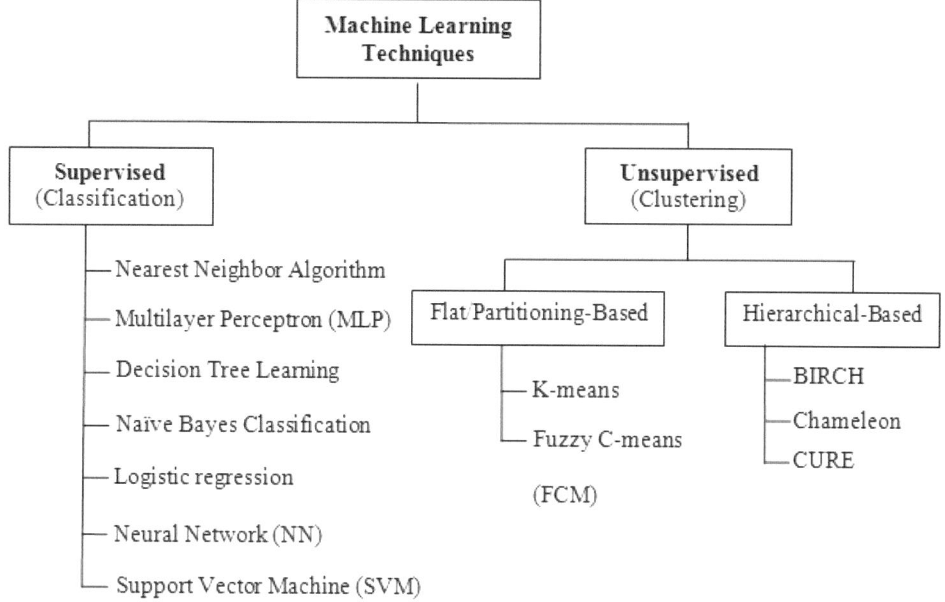

Figure 2. Classification of machine learning techniques.

length of trajectory, acceleration at start, midstrok pressure, midstrok finger area, mean pressure, and mean finger area. The author used support vector machine (SVM) as a classifier, and data analysis was done using WEKA software tool. The result in authentication of equal error rate (EER) was improved from single swipe (4%) to five swipes (0.2%).

Ref. [48] implemented a simple and efficient dynamic user authentication method. Authors also developed the data collection software that runs as the background job and without affecting other applications. This software has extracted the features such as click elapsed time, movement speed, movement acceleration, and relative position of extreme speed and used support vector machine (SVM) technique for classification of the data. This approach achieved the acceptable level of performance with false acceptance rate (FAR) of 0.37% and false rejection rate (FRR) of 1.12%.

Ref. [9] introduced a verification system based on mouse movements using logging tool recording user input (RUI). This system is able to verify a user accurately using newly defined angle-based metrics such as direction, angle of curvature, and curvature distance. This paper used support vector machine (SVM) on the design of the classifier user verification process. Around 30 users participated in this experiment. During their routine computing activities, the mouse movement data were recorded continuously. The result in an EER was recorded at 1.3%.

Ref. [51] used a mouse dynamic dataset from ISOT research lab (University of Victoria). This paper has applied Learning Algorithm for Multivariate Data Analysis (LAMDA) for data analysis. The evaluation of accuracy using 48 users achieved a FAR of 0% and a FRR of 0.36%.

Ref. [6] presented a static approach in which the user needs to perform a task called "follow the maze." Then, mouse movements are recorded to compute the velocity for X and Y directions. In the verification phase, edit distance (also called Levenshtein distance or dynamic time warping) is used for the purpose of comparison between training and testing dataset. Experiment was conducted involving 28 participants including people highly skilled in computer and people not so skillful in using a mouse device. Nevertheless, they are set to use the same mouse device during the experiment. The result for EER was measured at around 27%.

Ref. [5] presented a continuous user authentication approach with higher-level actions, and the characteristics recorded are distance, action type, direction, and duration. The parameters that are involved in this research were movement speed, direction of movement, type of action, traveled distance, and movement elapsed time. The main experiment involved 22 participants, and 284 hours of raw data are collected over 998 sessions. This paper has applied artificial neural network for the classification of data. The result was presented using receiver operating characteristic (ROC) curves and a confusion matrix yield at the crossover point. This approach achieved the accuracy with FAR of 2.4649% and FRR of 2.4614%.

Ref. [52] proposed a static authentication which presented an enrollment by moving the mouse toward the dots drawn sequentially on the screen. Besides, the user's mouse movements were computed to generate features for enrolment signature. During verification process, the user follows the dots pattern identical to that of an enrolment phase. Then, this value was compared with the enrollment signature. This experiment involved 15 users, and they must use the same computer and mouse. The equal error rate (EER) for this system was recorded at 15%.

Ref. [45] presented a system that is related to the continuous approach in which raw mouse data was preprocessed to build a model of a user's behavior. The raw features such as speed, distance, frequency, and angle were extracted to compute the mean, standard deviation, and third-moment values for N data points. This paper has applied a supervised learning method, a decision tree algorithm for classification. This algorithm provides an intelligible representation to discriminate among K users for decision-making process. An authentication experiment was participated by 11 users. They were instructed to run Internet Explorer using their own personal computer. The result achieved for an average false acceptance rate (FAR) was 0.43%, and an average false rejection rate (FRR) was 1.75%.

Ref. [44] introduced an approach for providing secure access over the Internet using biometric authentication. The system used a hybrid approach, which was the combination of keyboard and signature to ensure that the set of credentials supplied to the system at the login stage is genuine. In this experiment, the author developed a web-based applet for the collection of data. For keyboard, the parameters that involved were latency times and hold times, while for signature, the parameters used were angle and distance. This paper was applied in neural network for data analysis. The evaluation of accuracy achieved a FAR of 4.4% and a FRR of 0.2%.

Table 5 shows a list of recent works on different behavioral-based biometric authentication approach that includes the collection of data, the parameter measured, the data analysis, the software used, and the measurement of accuracy. The false rejection rate (FRR), false acceptance rate (FAR), and equal error rate (EER) for every approach are also investigated. Briefly, many

Author	Biometric approach	Data collection	Parameter (feature extraction)	Data analysis (classifier)	Software used	Measurement of accuracy
[47]	Touch swipes	Android (psychological questionnaire)	**Raw data:** touch action; X and Y coordinate; X, Y, and Z gravity; pressure exerted; and finger area **Feature vector:** duration, length of trajectory, average velocity, acceleration at start, midstrok pressure, midstrok finger area, mean pressure, mean finger area, mean X, mean Y, and mean Z	SVM	WEKA	EER
[48]	Mouse dynamics	Data collection software	**Feature vector:** click elapsed time, movement speed, movement acceleration, and relative position of extreme speed	SVM	Pattern-growth-based mining method	FAR, FRR
[9]	Mouse movement	Recording user input (RUI)	**Raw data: action type,** time stamp, coordinate X, and coordinate Y **Feature vector:** three fine-grained angle-based metrics (direction, angle of curvature, and curvature distance)	SVM	—	EER
[51]	Mouse dynamics	ISOT mouse dataset	Movement speed, direction of movement, type of action, traveled distance, and movement elapsed time	Learning Algorithm for Multivariate Data Analysis (LAMDA)	MATLAB	FAR, FRR
[6]	Mouse dynamics	GUI	**Feature vector:** horizontal and vertical track velocity	Edit distance metrics	—	EER
[5]	Mouse dynamics	The client software	**Feature vector:** movement speed, direction of movement, type of action, traveled distance, and movement elapsed time	Neural network	MATLAB	FAR, FRR
[52]	Mouse movement	GUI	**Feature vector:** speed, deviation, positive angle, and negative angle (average, SD, minimum, maximum)	Comparing value with the range of the user's counter value (exact value)	—	EER
[45]	Mouse dynamics	Mouse dynamic application	**Raw data:** speed, distance, frequency, and angle **Feature vector:** mean, standard deviation, and third-moment values for N data points	Decision tree algorithm	—	FAR, FRR

Author	Biometric approach	Data collection	Parameter (feature extraction)	Data analysis (classifier)	Software used	Measurement of accuracy
[44]	Hybrid approach (keyboard + signature)	Web-based applet	**Keyboard:** latency times and hold times **Signature:** angle and distance (two approaches used to extract—ranking approach and genetic approach)	Neural network	—	FAR, FRR

Table 5. Comparison of related works for behavioral-based biometric authentication.

classifier techniques have been developed in biometric authentication fields such as neural network, decision tree algorithm, Learning Algorithm for Multivariate Data Analysis (LAMDA), and SVM. However, there is still room to enhance the accuracy of FAR and FRR in this field.

4. Discussion

Nowadays, the knowledge-based methods are commonly used because they are simple, economic, and convenient mechanisms to be used and implemented. However, these methods are also known as being an extremely poor form of protection. There are several ways in which an impostor can attack password-protected systems. The most common form of attack is password guessing. Authentication can also use something that user has as alternatives such as tokens, smart card, and QR code. However, these approaches does not lend itself particularly well in the above situation either. These kinds of approaches are more secure to use than a user's PIN or password. Thus, this possession-based method for user authentication can be considered weaker still. To overcome the drawbacks of those authentication methods, research has been shifted into biometric-based methods for the purposes of authentication, as biometric characteristics are not possible for sharing and repudiating due to uniqueness. Behavioral biometrics is the field of study related to the measure of uniquely identifying measurable patterns in human activities. The term contrasts with physical *biometrics*, which involves innate human characteristics such as fingerprints or iris patterns. **Table 6** shows the user authentication method that can be generally categorized into four categories.

Method	Instances	Properties
Something the user knows	PIN, password, etc.	Can be shared and forgotten
Something the user has	Token, smart card, QR code, etc.	Can be lost and duplicated
Something the user is	Finger scan, iris scan, retina scan, hand scan, facial scan, etc.	Not possible to share and repudiate
Something the user exhibits	Signature, gaits (the way humans walk), keystroke dynamics (typing styles), mouse dynamics, etc.	Not possible to share and repudiate

Table 6. Methodologies of user authentication.

In reality, many behavioral-based biometric methods have been proposed. However, the implementation and deployment are still lacking due to a few reasons such as costly devices, difficult to implement, and sometimes lack of accuracy.

5. Conclusion

This survey provides a comprehensive study on machine learning techniques in the domain of behavioral-based biometric authentication. Particularly, we reassess papers published between the years 2003 and 2016. First, we introduce the concept of biometric authentication and its application. Second, we present the taxonomy of authentication methods with detailed discussion on knowledge-based, possession-based, and biometrics-based methods. In the section of behavioral-based biometric authentication, we discuss the two subcategories of machine learning techniques which are supervised (classification) and unsupervised (clustering) techniques. We investigate each subcategory that has been implemented in the previous behavioral-based biometric authentication. In the end of this paper, we should be able to acquire relevant knowledge required for enhancing the performance of the behavioral-based biometric authentication.

Acknowledgements

This research was supported by the Malaysian Ministry of Higher Education [Grant No. FRGS/1/2017/ICT03/UNISZA/02/1 (RR228)].

Conflict of interest

All authors agreed that there is no conflict of interests.

Author details

Nurul Afnan Mahadi, Mohamad Afendee Mohamed*, Amirul Ihsan Mohamad, Mokhairi Makhtar, Mohd Fadzil Abdul Kadir and Mustafa Mamat

*Address all correspondence to: mafendee@unisza.edu.my

Faculty of Informatics and Computing, Universiti Sultan Zainal Abidin, Besut, Malaysia

References

[1] Kissel R. Glossary of Key Information Security Terms. Maryland: National Institute of Standards and Technology; 2013. DOI: 10.6028/NIST.IR.7298r2

[2] Stapleton JJ. Security without Obscurity: A Guide to Confidentiality, Authentication, and Integrity. Boca Raton: CRC Press; 2014

[3] Clarke N. Transparent User Authentication: Biometrics, RFID and Behavioural Profiling. London: Springer Science & Business Media; 2011

[4] CNSS. Committee on National Security Systems (CNSS). Glossary, CNSSI No. 4009. April 6, 2015. Available from: https://cryptosmith.files.wordpress.com/2015/08/glossary-2015-cnss.pdf

[5] Ahmed AAE, Traore I. A new biometric technology based on mouse dynamics. IEEE Transactions on Dependable and Secure Computing. 2007;**4**(3):165-179

[6] Bours P, Fullu CJ. A login system using mouse dynamics. In: IIH-MSP 2009-2009 5th International Conference on Intelligent Information Hiding and Multimedia Signal Processing; 2009, pp. 1072-1077

[7] Jorgensen Z, Yu T. On mouse dynamics as a behavioral biometric for authentication. In: Proceedings of the 6th ACM Symposium on Information, Computer and Communications Security– ASIACCS '11; 2011. pp. 476

[8] Gorodnichy DO. Evolution and evaluation of biometric systems. In: Proceedings of the 2009 IEEE Symposium on Computational Intelligence in Security and Defense Applications (CISDA 2009) Evolution, (Cisda); 2009

[9] Zheng N, Paloski A, Wang, H. An efficient user verification system via mouse movements. In: Proceedings of the 18th ACM Conference on Computer and Communications Security; 2011. pp. 139-150

[10] Vongsingthong S, Boonkrong S. A survey on smartphone authentication. Walailak Journal of Science and Technology. 2015;**12**(1):1-19

[11] Sahu SB, Singh A. Survey on various techniques of user authentication and graphical password. International Journal of Computer Trends and Technology (IJCTT). 2014; **16**(3):98-102

[12] Bhanushali A, Mange B, Vyas H, Bhanushali H, Bhogle P. Comparison of graphical password authentication techniques. International Journal of Computer Applications. 2015;**116**(1):975-8887

[13] Rittenhouse RG, Chaudhry JA. A survey of alternative authentication methods. In: International Conference on Recent Advances in Computer Systems, (Racs 2015); 2015. pp. 218-220

[14] Saifan R, Salem A, Zaidan D, Swidan A. A survey of behavioral authentication using keystroke dynamics: Touch screens and mobile devices. Journal of Social Sciences. 2016;**55**(11):29-41

[15] Jesudoss A, Subramaniam NP. A survey on authentication attacks and countermeasures. Indian Journal of Computer Science and Engineering (IJCSE). 2014;**5**(2):71-77

[16] Von Zezschwitz E, Koslow A, De Luca A, Hussmann H. Making graphic-based authentication secure against smudge attacks. In: Proceedings of the 2013 International Conference on Intelligent User Interfaces–IUI '13; 2013. pp. 277

[17] Kim H, Lee K, Jung, Y. A design of authentication strengthening scheme using matrix values of image in smart phone environment. In: Proceedings of the 1st International Conference on Convergence and It's Application, 24; 2013. pp. 179-182

[18] Takamizawa H, Tanaka N. Authentication system using location information on ipad or smartphone. International Journal of Computer Theory and Engineering. 2012;**4**(2):153-157

[19] Nickel C. Accelerometer-Based Biometric Gait Recognition for Authentication on Smartphones [Doctoral dissertation]. Technische Universität; 2012

[20] Khan WZ, Aalsalem MY, Xiang Y. A graphical password based system for small mobile devices. IJCSI International Journal of Computer Science Issues. 2011;**8**(5):145-154

[21] Bojinov H, Boneh D. Mobile Token-based authentication on a budget. In: Proceedings of the 12th Workshop on Mobile Computing Systems and Applications - HotMobile '11; 2011. pp. 14

[22] Ghogare SD, Jadhav SP, Chadha AR, Patil HC. Location based authentication: A new approach towards providing security. International Journal of Scientific and Research Publications. 2012;**2**(1):2250-3153

[23] Bianchi A, Oakley I, Kwon DS. Using mobile device screens for authentication. In: Proceedings of the 23rd Australian Computer-Human interaction conference, OzCHI 2011; 2011. pp. 50-53

[24] Lakshmi P, Susan V. Biometric authentication using ElGamal cryptosystem and DNA sequence. International Journal of Engineering Science and Technology. 2010; **2**(6):1993-1996

[25] Prabhakar S, Pankanti S, Jain AK. Biometric recognition: Security and privacy concerns. IEEE Security & Privacy Magazine. 2003;**1**(2):33-42

[26] Stein C, Nickel C, Busch C. Fingerphoto recognition with smartphone cameras. In: Proceedings of the International Conference of the Biometrics Special Interst Group; 2012. pp. 1-12

[27] Gupta P, Wee TK, Ramasubbu N, Lo D, Gao D, Balan RK. HuMan: Creating memorable fingerprints of mobile users. In: IEEE International Conference on Pervasive Computing and Communications Workshops, PERCOM Workshops 2012, (March); 2012. pp. 479-482

[28] Cheng K, Kumar A. contactless finger knuckle identification using smartphones. In: Proceedings of the International Conference of the Biometrics Special Interest Group 2012; 2012. pp. 1-6

[29] Hu JY, Sueng CC, Liao WH, Ho CC. Android-based mobile payment service protected by 3-factor authentication and virtual private Ad Hoc Networking. In: 2012 Computing, Communications and Applications Conference (ComComAp 2012); 2012. Vol. 1. pp. 111-116

[30] Hernandez CP, Torres-Huitzil C. A fragile watermarking scheme for image authentication in mobile devices. In: Electrical Engineering Computing Science and Automatic Control (CCE), 2011 8th International Conference on (pp. 1-6). IEEE; 2011. pp. 39-43

[31] Somnath D, Samanta D. Improved feature processing for iris biometric authentication system. International Journal of Computer Systems Science and Engineering (IJCSSE), World Academy of Science. 2010;**4**(3):455-462

[32] Babich A. Biometric authentication. Types of Biometric Identifiers. 2012:1-56

[33] Lin C, Liang D, Chang CC, Yang CH. A new non-intrusive authentication method based on the orientation sensor for smartphone users. In: 2012 IEEE Sixth International Conference on Software Security and Reliability; 2012. pp. 245-252

[34] Nickel C, Wirtl T, Busch, C. Authentication of smartphone users based on the way they walk using k-NN algorithm. In: 2012 Eighth IEEE International Conference on Intelligent Information Hiding and Multimedia Signal Processing (IIH-MSP); 2012. pp. 16-20

[35] Shen P, Jin A, Tee C, Song T. Expert systems with applications keystroke dynamics in password authentication enhancement. Expert Systems with Applications. 2010; **37**(12):8618-8627

[36] Giot R, El-abed M, Hemery B, Rosenberger C. Unconstrained keystroke dynamics authentication with shared secret. Computers and Security. 2011;**30**(6-7):427-445

[37] Giot R, El-Abed M, Rosenberger, C. Keystroke dynamics authentication for collaborative systems. In: 2009 International Symposium on Collaborative Technologies and Systems, CTS 2009; 2009. pp. 172-179. https://doi.org/10.1109/CTS.2009.5067478

[38] Bartlow N, Cukic B. Evaluating the reliability of credential hardening through keystroke dynamics. In: IEEE 17th International Symposium in Software Reliability Engineering, 2006. (ISSRE'06); 2006. pp. 117-126

[39] Justino EJR, Bortolozzi F, Sabourin R. A comparison of SVM and HMM classifiers in the off-line signature verification. Pattern Recognition Letters. 2005;**26**:1377-1385

[40] Hanmandlu M, Hafizuddin M, Yusof M, Krishna V. Off-line signature verification and forgery detection using fuzzy modeling. Pattern Recognition. 2005;**38**:341-356

[41] Ajufor N, Amalraj A, Diaz R, Islam M, Lampe M. Refinement of a mouse movement biometric system. In: Proceedings of Student-Faculty Research Day, CSIS, Pace University, May 2nd, 2008; 2008, pp. 1-8

[42] Buriro A, Crispo B, Delfrari F, Wrona K. Hold & Sign: A novel behavioral biometrics for smartphone user authentication Hold & Sign: A novel behavioral biometrics for smartphone user authentication. In: IEEE Security and Privacy Workshops MoST 2016, (MAY); 2016

[43] Xiao G, Milanova M, Xie M. Secure behavioral biometric authentication with leap motion. In: 4th International Symposium on Digital Forensics and Security, ISDFS 2016–Proceeding; 2016. pp. 112-118

[44] Everitt RAJ, McOwan PW. Java-based internet biometric authentication system. IEEE Transactions on Pattern Analysis and Machine Intelligence. 2003;**25**(9):1166-1172

[45] Pusara M, Brodley CE. User re-authentication via mouse movements. In: Proceedings of the 2004 ACM Workshop on Visualization and Data Mining for Computer Security VizSECDMSEC 04; 2004. pp. 1-8

[46] Hamid NA, Safei S, Dhalila S, Satar M, Chuprat S, Ahmad R. Randomized mouse movement for behavioral biometric identification. International Journal of Interactive Digital Media. 2013;**1**(2):52-57

[47] Antal M, Szabó LZ. Biometric authentication based on touchscreen swipe patterns. Procedia Technology. 2016;**22**(October 2015):862-869

[48] Shen C, Cai Z, Guan X. Continuous authentication for mouse dynamics: A pattern-growth approach. In: Proceedings of the International Conference on Dependable Systems and Networks; 2012

[49] Fahad A, Alshatri N, Tari Z, Alamri A, Khalil I, Zomaya A, et al. A survey of clustering algorithms for big data: Taxonomy & empirical analysis. IEEE Transactions on Emerging Topics in Computing. 2014

[50] Berkhin P. A survey of clustering data mining. In: Grouping Multidimensional Data. Berlin Heidelberg: Springer; 2006. pp. 25-71

[51] Nakkabi Y, Traoré I, Ahmed AAE. Improving mouse dynamics biometric performance using variance reduction via extractors with separate features. IEEE Transactions on Systems, Man and Cybernetics. 2010;**40**(6):1345-1353

[52] Hashia S, Pollett C, Stamp M, Hall M, Jose S. On using mouse movements as a biometric. In: Proceeding in the International Conference on Computer Science and Its Applications; 2005. Vol. 1